Evangelism & the Sovereignty of God

J. I. Packer

InterVarsity Press
Downers Grove, Illinois 60515

Fifth American printing, May 1974,
by InterVarsity Press with
permission from Inter-Varsity
Fellowship. All rights reserved.
No part of this book may be reproduced
in any form without written
permission from InterVarsity Press.

InterVarsity Press is the book
publishing division of Inter-Varsity
Christian Fellowship, a student
movement active on campus at
hundreds of universities, colleges and
schools of nursing. For information
about this dynamic association, write
IVCF, 233 Langdon, Madison,
WI 53703. If you're a student, four
chances out of five you'll find a local
IVCF chapter on your campus.

ISBN 0-87784-680-4
Library of Congress Catalog
Card Number: 67-28875

Printed in the United
States of America

CONTENTS

FOREWORD

THE nucleus of the following discourse was an address given at the Pre-Mission Conference of the London Inter-Faculty Christian Union on October 24th, 1959. It has been expanded in the hope of giving it a wider usefulness. Its origin, and the practical nature of its subject-matter, accounts for its homiletical style.

Lest its purpose be misconceived, may I say at the outset what it is not.

It is not a blueprint for evangelistic action today, though it sets out relevant principles for determining any evangelistic strategy.

It is not a contribution to the current controversy about modern evangelistic methods, though it lays down relevant principles for settling that controversy.

It is not a critique of the evangelistic principles of any particular person or persons, though it provides relevant principles for evaluating all evangelistic activities.

What is it, then? It is a piece of biblical and theological reasoning, designed to clarify the relationship between three realities: God's sovereignty, man's responsibility, and the Christian's evangelistic duty. The last of these is its proper subject; divine sovereignty and human responsibility are discussed only so far as they bear on evangelism. The aim of the discourse is to dispel the suspicion (current, it seems, in some quarters) that faith in the absolute sovereignty of God hinders a full recognition and acceptance of evangelistic responsibility, and to show that, on the contrary, only this faith can give Christians the strength that they need to fulfil their evangelistic task.

It must not be thought that on all the points with which I deal I am trying to lay down some sort of 'I.V.F. orthodoxy'. The limits of 'I.V.F. orthodoxy' are set out in the Fellowship's doctrinal basis. Beyond those limits, members of the Fellowship are free, in John Wesley's phrase, to 'think and let think', and no opinion on any subject can be regarded as the only one permissible. On the subject now to be dealt with, it may well be that some members of the Fellowship will think differently from the present writer. Equally, however, an author has a right to his own opinion, and he cannot be expected to conceal his views when he believes them to be biblical, relevant, and (in the strict sense) edifying.

J. I. PACKER

INTRODUCTION

ALWAYS and everywhere the servants of Christ are under orders to evangelize, and I hope that what I shall say now will act as an incentive to this task. I hope, too, that it will serve a further purpose. There is in Christian circles at the present time much heart-searching and dispute about ways and means of evangelism. I want to speak about the spiritual factors involved in evangelizing, and I hope that what I say may help towards resolving some of the current disagreements and debates.

Evangelism is my proper subject, and I am to speak of it in relation to the sovereignty of God. That means that I shall not be speaking of the sovereignty of God further than is necessary for right thinking about evangelism. Divine sovereignty is a vast subject: it embraces everything that comes into the biblical picture of God as Lord and King in His world, the One who 'worketh all things after the counsel of his own will' (Eph. i.11), directing every process and ordering every event for the fulfilling of His own eternal plan. To deal with such a subject in full, one would have to take soundings in the depths, not merely of providence, but also of predestination and the last things, and that is more than we can or need do here. The only aspect of divine

sovereignty that will concern us in these pages is
God's sovereignty in grace : His almighty action in
bringing helpless sinners home through Christ to
Himself.

In examining the relationship between God's
sovereignty and the Christian's task of evangelism,
I have a specific aim in view. There is abroad today
a widespread suspicion that a robust faith in the
absolute sovereignty of God is bound to undermine
any adequate sense of human responsibility. Such a
faith is thought to be dangerous to spiritual health,
because it breeds a habit of complacent inertia. In
particular, it is thought to paralyse evangelism by
robbing one both of the motive to evangelize and of
the message to evangelize with. The supposition
seems to be that you cannot evangelize effectively
unless you are prepared to pretend while you are
doing it that the doctrine of divine sovereignty is not
true. I shall try to make it evident that this is nonsense. I shall try to show further that, so far from
inhibiting evangelism, faith in the sovereignty of
God's government and grace is the only thing that
can sustain it, for it is the only thing that can give
us the resilience that we need if we are to evangelize
boldly and persistently, and not be daunted by
temporary setbacks. So far from being weakened
by this faith, therefore, evangelism will inevitably
be weak and lack staying power without it. This, I
hope, will become clear as we proceed.

CHAPTER I

DIVINE SOVEREIGNTY

I DO not intend to spend any time at all proving to you the general truth that *God is sovereign in His world*. There is no need; for I know that, if you are a Christian, you believe this already. How do I know that? Because I know that, if you are a Christian, you pray; and the recognition of God's sovereignty is the basis of your prayers. In prayer, you ask for things and give thanks for things. Why? Because you recognize that God is the author and source of all the good that you have had already, and all the good that you hope for in the future. This is the fundamental philosophy of Christian prayer. The prayer of a Christian is not an attempt to force God's hand, but a humble acknowledgment of helplessness and dependence. When we are on our knees, we know that it is not we who control the world; it is not in our power, therefore, to supply our needs by our own independent efforts; every good thing that we desire for ourselves and for others must be sought from God, and will come, if it comes at all, as a gift from His hands. If this is true even of our daily bread (and the Lord's Prayer teaches us that it is), much more is it true of spiritual benefits. This is all luminously clear to us when we are actually praying, whatever we may be betrayed into saying in argument afterwards. In effect, therefore,

what we do every time we pray is to confess our
own impotence and God's sovereignty. The very fact
that a Christian prays is thus proof positive that he
believes in the Lordship of his God.

Nor, again, am I going to spend time proving to
you the particular truth that *God is sovereign in
salvation.* For that, too, you believe already. Two
facts show this. In the first place, you give God
thanks for your conversion. Now why do you do
that? Because you know in your heart that God was
entirely responsible for it. You did not save yourself;
He saved you. Your thanksgiving is itself an acknowledgment that your conversion was not your own
work, but His work. You do not put it down to
chance or accident that you came under Christian
influence when you did. You do not put it down to
chance or accident that you attended a Christian
church, that you heard the Christian gospel, that
you had Christian friends and, perhaps, a Christian
home, that the Bible fell into your hands, that you
saw your need of Christ and came to trust Him as
your Saviour. You do not attribute your repenting
and believing to your own wisdom, or prudence, or
sound judgment, or good sense. Perhaps, in the days
when you were seeking Christ, you laboured and
strove hard, read and pondered much, but all that
outlay of effort did not make your conversion your
own work. Your act of faith when you closed with
Christ was yours in the sense that it was you who
performed it; but that does not mean that you saved
yourself. In fact, it never occurs to you to suppose
that you saved yourself.

As you look back, you take to yourself the blame for your past blindness and indifference and obstinacy and evasiveness in face of the gospel message; but you do not pat yourself on the back for having been at length mastered by the insistent Christ. You would never dream of dividing the credit for your salvation between God and yourself. You have never for one moment supposed that the decisive contribution to your salvation was yours and not God's. You have never told God that, while you are grateful for the means and opportunities of grace that He gave you, you realize that you have to thank, not Him, but yourself for the fact that you responded to His call. Your heart revolts at the very thought of talking to God in such terms. In fact, you thank Him no less sincerely for the gift of faith and repentance than for the gift of a Christ to trust and turn to. This is the way in which, since you became a Christian, your heart has always led you. You give God all the glory for all that your salvation involved, and you know that it would be blasphemy if you refused to thank Him for bringing you to faith. Thus, in the way that you think of your conversion and give thanks for your conversion, you acknowledge the sovereignty of divine grace. And every other Christian in the world does the same.

It is instructive in this connection to ponder Charles Simeon's account of his conversation with John Wesley on Dec. 20th, 1784 (the date is given in Wesley's *Journal*): ' "Sir, I understand that you are called an Arminian; and I have been sometimes called a Calvinist; and therefore I suppose we are to draw daggers. But before I consent to begin the combat, with your permission I will ask you a few questions. . . . Pray, Sir, do you feel yourself a depraved creature, so depraved that you would never have thought of turning to God, if God had not first put it into your heart?" "Yes," says the veteran, "I do indeed." "And do you utterly despair of recommending yourself to God by anything you can do; and look for salvation solely through the blood and righteousness of Christ?" "Yes, solely through Christ." "But, Sir, supposing you were at first saved by Christ, are you not somehow or other to save yourself afterwards by your own works?" "No, I must be saved by Christ from first to last." "Allowing, then, that you were first turned by the grace of God, are you not in some way or other to keep yourself by your own power?" "No." "What, then, are you to be upheld every hour and every moment by God, as much as an infant in its mother's arms?" "Yes, altogether." "And is all your hope in the grace and mercy of God to preserve you unto His heavenly kingdom?" "Yes, I have no hope but in Him." "Then, Sir, with your leave I will put up my dagger again; for this is all my Calvinism; this is my election, my justification by faith, my final perseverance : it is in substance all that I hold, and as I hold it; and therefore, if you please, instead of searching out terms and phrases to be a ground of contention between us, we will cordially unite in those things wherein we agree." "[1]

There is a second way in which you acknowledge

[1] *Horae Homileticae*, Preface : I. xvii f.

that God is sovereign in salvation. You pray for the conversion of others. In what terms, now, do you intercede for them? Do you limit yourself to asking that God will bring them to a point where they can save themselves, independently of Him? I do not think you do. I think that what you do is to pray in categorical terms that God will, quite simply and decisively, save them: that He will open the eyes of their understanding, soften their hard hearts, renew their natures, and move their wills to receive the Saviour. You ask God to work in them everything necessary for their salvation. You would not dream of making it a point in your prayer that you are not asking God actually to bring them to faith, because you recognize that that is something He cannot do. Nothing of the sort! When you pray for unconverted people, you do so on the assumption that it is in God's power to bring them to faith. You entreat Him to do that very thing, and your confidence in asking rests upon the certainty that He is able to do what you ask. And so indeed He is: this conviction, which animates your intercessions, is God's own truth, written on your heart by the Holy Spirit. In prayer, then (and the Christian is at his sanest and wisest when he prays), you *know* that it is God who saves men; you *know* that what makes men turn to God is God's own gracious work of drawing them to Himself; and the content of your prayers is determined by this knowledge. Thus, by your practice of intercession, no less than by giving thanks for your conversion, you acknowledge and confess the sov-

ereignty of God's grace. And so do all Christian
people everywhere.

There is a long-standing controversy in the Church
as to whether God is really Lord in relation to human
conduct and saving faith or not. What has been said
shows us how we should regard this controversy.
The situation is not what it seems to be. For it is
not true that some Christians believe in divine sovereignty while others hold an opposite view. What
is true is that all Christians believe in divine sovereignty, but some are not aware that they do, and
mistakenly imagine and insist that they reject it.
What causes this odd state of affairs? The root
cause is the same as in most cases of error in the
Church—the intruding of rationalistic speculations,
the passion for systematic consistency, a reluctance
to recognize the existence of mystery and to let God
be wiser than men, and a consequent subjecting of
Scripture to the supposed demands of human logic.
People see that the Bible teaches man's responsibility
for his actions; they do not see (man, indeed, cannot
see) how this is consistent with the sovereign Lordship of God over those actions. They are not content
to let the two truths live side by side, as they do in
the Scriptures, but jump to the conclusion that, in
order to uphold the biblical truth of human responsibility, they are bound to reject the equally biblical
and equally true doctrine of divine sovereignty,
and to explain away the great number of texts that
teach it. The desire to over-simplify the Bible by cut-
ting out the mysteries is natural to our perverse
minds, and it is not surprising that even good men

should fall victim to it. Hence this persistent and troublesome dispute. The irony of the situation, however, is that when we ask how the two sides pray, it becomes apparent that those who profess to deny God's sovereignty really believe in it just as strongly as those who affirm it.

How, then, do you pray? Do you ask God for your daily bread? Do you thank God for your conversion? Do you pray for the conversion of others? If the answer is 'no', I can only say that I do not think you are yet born again. But if the answer is 'yes'—well, that proves that, whatever side you may have taken in debates on this question in the past, in your heart you believe in the sovereignty of God no less firmly than anyone else. On our feet we may have arguments about it, but on our knees we are all agreed. And it is this common agreement, of which our prayers give proof, that I take as our starting-point now.

CHAPTER II

DIVINE SOVEREIGNTY AND HUMAN RESPONSIBILITY

OUR aim in the present study is to think out the nature of the Christian's evangelistic task in the light of this agreed presupposition that God is sovereign in salvation. Now, we need to recognize right at the outset that this is no easy assignment. All theological topics contain pitfalls for the unwary, for God's truth is never quite what man would have expected; and our present subject is more treacherous than most. This is because in thinking it through we have to deal with an *antinomy* in the biblical revelation, and in such circumstances our finite, fallen minds are more than ordinarily apt to go astray.

What is an antinomy? *The Shorter Oxford Dictionary* defines it as 'a contradiction between conclusions which seem equally logical, reasonable or necessary'. For our purposes, however, this definition is not quite accurate; the opening words should read 'an *appearance* of contradiction'. For the whole point of an antinomy—in theology, at any rate—is that it is not a real contradiction, though it looks like one. It is an *apparent* incompatibility between two apparent truths. An antinomy exists when a pair of principles stand side by side, seemingly irreconcilable, yet both undeniable. There are cogent reasons

for believing each of them; each rests on clear and
solid evidence; but it is a mystery to you how they
can be squared with each other. You see that each
must be true on its own, but you do not see how they
can both be true together. Let me give an example. Modern physics faces an antinomy, in this
sense, in its study of light. There is cogent evidence
to show that light consists of waves, and equally
cogent evidence to show that it consists of particles.
It is not apparent how light can be both waves and
particles, but the evidence is there, and so neither
view can be ruled out in favour of the other. Neither,
however, can be reduced to the other or explained
in terms of the other; the two seemingly incompatible positions must be held together, and both must
be treated as true. Such a necessity scandalizes our
tidy minds, no doubt, but there is no help for it if
we are to be loyal to the facts.

It appears, therefore, that an antinomy is not the
same thing as a paradox. A paradox is a figure of
speech, a play on words. It is a form of statement
that seems to unite two opposite ideas, or to deny
something by the very terms in which it is asserted.
Many truths about the Christian life can be expressed as paradoxes. A Prayer Book collect, for
instance, declares that God's 'service is perfect free-
dom' : man goes free through becoming a slave. Paul
states various paradoxes of his own Christian experience : 'sorrowful, yet always rejoicing . . . having
nothing, and yet possessing all things'; 'when I am
weak, then am I strong' (2 Cor. vi.10, xii.10). The
point of a paradox, however, is that what creates the

appearance of contradiction is not the facts, but the
words. The contradiction is verbal, but not real,
and a little thought shows how it can be eliminated
and the same idea expressed in non-paradoxical
form. In other words a paradox is always *dispensable*.
Look at the examples quoted. The Prayer Book might
have said that those who serve God are free from
sin's dominion. In 2 Cor. vi. 10 Paul might have said
that sorrow at circumstances, and joy in God, are
constantly combined in his experience, and that,
though he owns no property and has no bank
balance, there is a sense in which everything belongs
to him, because he is Christ's, and Christ is Lord of
all. Again, in 2 Cor. xii. 10, he might have said that
the Lord strengthens him most when he is most
conscious of his natural infirmity. Such non-paradoxical forms of speech are clumsy and dull
beside the paradoxes which they would replace, but
they express precisely the same meaning. For a paradox is merely a matter of how you use words; the
employment of paradox is an arresting trick of
speech, but it does not imply even an appearance of
contradiction in the facts that you are describing.

Also it should be noted that a paradox is always
comprehensible. A speaker or writer casts his ideas
into paradoxes in order to make them memorable
and provoke thought about them. But the person at
the receiving end must be able, on reflection, to see
how to unravel the paradox, otherwise it will seem
to him to be really self-contradictory, and therefore
really meaningless. An incomprehensible paradox
could not be distinguished from a mere contradiction

in terms. Sheer paradox would thus have to be
written off as sheer nonsense.

By contrast, however, an antinomy is neither dispensable nor comprehensible. It is not a figure of
speech, but an observed relation between two statements of fact. It is not deliberately manufactured;
it is forced upon us by the facts themselves. It is
unavoidable, and it is insoluble. We do not invent it,
and we cannot explain it. Nor is there any way to
get rid of it, save by falsifying the very facts that led
us to it.

What should one do, then, with an antinomy?
Accept it for what it is, and learn to live with it.
Refuse to regard the apparent inconsistency as real;
put down the semblance of contradiction to the
deficiency of your own understanding; think of the
two principles as, not rival alternatives, but, in some
way that at present you do not grasp, complementary to each other. Be careful, therefore, not to set
them at loggerheads, nor to make deductions from
either that would cut across the other (such deductions would, for that very reason, be certainly un-
sound). Use each within the limits of its own sphere
of reference (*i.e.*, the area delimited by the evidence
from which the principle has been drawn). Note
what connections exist between the two truths and
their two frames of reference, and teach yourself
to think of reality in a way that provides for their
peaceful coexistence, remembering that reality itself
has proved actually to contain them both. This is
how antinomies must be handled, whether in nature
or in Scripture. This, as I understand it, is how

modern physics deals with the problem of light, and this is how Christians have to deal with the antinomies of biblical teaching.

The particular antinomy which concerns us here is the apparent opposition between divine sovereignty and human responsibility, or (putting it more biblically) between what God does as King and what He does as Judge. Scripture teaches that, as King, He orders and controls all things, human actions among them, in accordance with His own eternal purpose.[1] Scripture also teaches that, as Judge, He holds every man responsible for the choices he makes and the courses of action he pursues.[2] Thus, hearers of the gospel are responsible for their reaction; if they reject the good news, they are guilty of unbelief. 'He that believeth not is condemned already, because he hath not believed . . .'[3] Again, Paul, entrusted with the gospel, is responsible for preaching it; if he neglects his commission, he is penalized for unfaithfulness. 'Necessity is laid upon me; yea, woe is unto me, if I preach not the gospel!'[4] God's sovereignty and man's responsibility are taught us side by side in the same Bible; sometimes, indeed, in the same text.[5] Both are thus guaranteed to us by the same divine authority; both, therefore,

[1] See Gn. xlv.8, l.20; Pr. xvi.9, xxi.1; Mt. x.29; Acts iv.27f; Rom. ix.20 f.; Eph. i.11, etc.

[2] See Mt. xxv; Rom. ii.1–16; Rev. xx.11–13, etc.

[3] Jn. iii.18; cf. Mt. xi.20–24; Acts xiii.38–41; 2 Thes. i.7–10, etc.   [4] 1 Cor. ix.16; cf. Ezk. iii.17 ff., xxxiii.7 ff.

[5] E.g., Lk. xxii.22 : 'the Son of man goeth (to his death), as it was determined; but woe unto that man by whom he is betrayed!' Cf. Acts ii.23.

are true. It follows that they must be held together, and not played off against each other. Man is a responsible moral agent, though he is *also* divinely controlled; man is divinely controlled, though he is *also* a responsible moral agent. God's sovereignty is a reality, and man's responsibility is a reality too. This is the revealed antinomy in terms of which we have to do our thinking about evangelism.

To our finite minds, of course, the thing is inexplicable. It sounds like a contradiction, and our first reaction is to complain that it is absurd. Paul notices this complaint in Romans ix. 'Thou wilt say then unto me, Why does he (God) yet find fault? For who hath resisted his will?' (Rom. ix.19). If, as our Lord, God orders all our actions, how can it be reasonable or right for Him to act also as our Judge, and condemn our shortcomings? Observe how Paul replies. He does not attempt to demonstrate the propriety of God's action; instead, he rebukes the spirit of the question. 'Nay but, O man, who art thou that repliest against God?' What the objector has to learn is that he, a creature and a sinner, has no right whatsoever to find fault with the revealed ways of God. Creatures are not entitled to register complaints about their Creator. As Paul goes on to say, God's sovereignty is wholly just, for His right to dispose of His creatures is absolute.[6] Earlier in the Epistle, he had shown that God's judgment of sinners is also wholly just, since our sins richly deserve His sentence.[7] Our part, he would tell us, is to acknowledge these facts, and to adore God's

[6] Rom. ix.20 f.   [7] Rom. i.18 ff., 32, ii.1–16.

righteousness, both as King and as Judge; not to speculate as to how His just sovereignty can be consistent with His just judgment, and certainly not to call the justice of either in question because we find the problem of their relationship too hard for us! Our speculations are not the measure of our God. The Creator has told us that He is both a sovereign Lord and a righteous Judge, and that should be enough for us. Why do we hesitate to take His word for it? Can we not trust what He says?

We ought not in any case to be surprised when we find mysteries of this sort in God's Word. For the Creator is incomprehensible to His creatures. A God whom we could understand exhaustively, and whose revelation of Himself confronted us with no mysteries whatsoever, would be a God in man's image, and therefore an imaginary God, not the God of the Bible at all. For what the God of the Bible says is this: 'My thoughts are not your thoughts, neither are your ways my ways . . . as the heavens are higher than the earth, so are my ways higher than your ways, and my thoughts than your thoughts' (Is. lv. 8 f.). The antinomy which we face now is only one of a number that the Bible contains. We may be sure that they all find their reconciliation in the mind and counsel of God, and we may hope that in heaven we shall understand them ourselves. But meanwhile, our wisdom is to maintain with equal emphasis both the apparently conflicting truths in each case, to hold them together in the relation in which the Bible itself sets them, and to recognize that here is a mystery which we cannot expect to solve in this world.

This is easily said, but the thing is not easily done. For our minds dislike antinomies. We like to tie up everything into neat intellectual parcels, with all appearance of mystery dispelled and no loose ends hanging out. Hence we are tempted to get rid of antinomies from our minds by illegitimate means : to suppress, or jettison, one truth in the supposed interests of the other, and for the sake of a tidier theology. So it is in the present case. The temptation is to undercut and maim the one truth by the way in which we stress the other : to assert man's responsibility in a way that excludes God from being sovereign, or to affirm God's sovereignty in a way that destroys the responsibility of man. Both mistakes need to be guarded against. It is worth reflecting, therefore, on the way in which these temptations arise in connection specifically with evangelism.

There is, first, the temptation to *an exclusive concern with human responsibility.* As we have seen, human responsibility is a fact, and a very solemn fact. Man's responsibility to his Maker is, indeed, the fundamental fact of his life, and it can never be taken too seriously. God made us responsible moral agents, and He will not treat us as anything less. His Word addresses each of us individually, and each of us is responsible for the way in which he responds—for his attention or inattention, his belief or unbelief, his obedience or disobedience. We cannot evade responsibility for our reaction to God's revelation. We live under His law. We must answer to Him for our lives.

Man without Christ is a guilty sinner, answerable

to God for breaking His law. That is why he needs the gospel. When he hears the gospel, he is responsible for the decision that he makes about it. It sets before him a choice between life and death, the most momentous choice that any man can ever face. When we present the gospel to an unconverted man, it is very likely that, without fully realizing what he is doing, he will try to blind himself to the gravity of this issue, and thereby to justify himself in shrugging the whole thing off. Then we have to use every legitimate means in our power to bring home to him the seriousness of the choice that confronts him, and to urge him not to let himself treat so solemn a matter in an irresponsible way. When we preach the promises and invitations of the gospel, and offer Christ to sinful men and women, it is part of our task to emphasize and re-emphasize that they are responsible to God for the way in which they react to the good news of His grace. No preacher can ever make this point too strongly.

Similarly, we ourselves have a responsibility for making the gospel known. Christ's command to His disciples, 'Go ye . . . and make disciples . . .' (Mt. xxviii.19, RSV), was spoken to them in their representative capacity; this is Christ's command, not merely to the apostles, but to the whole Church. Evangelism is the inalienable responsibility of every Christian community, and every Christian man. We are all under orders to devote ourselves to spreading the good news, and to use all our ingenuity and enterprise to bring it to the notice of the whole world. The Christian, therefore, must constantly be searching his conscience, asking himself if he is doing all that he might be doing in this field. For this also is a responsibility that cannot be shrugged off.

It is necessary, therefore, to take the thought of human responsibility, as it affects both the preacher and the hearer of the gospel, very seriously indeed. But we must not let it drive the thought of divine sovereignty out of our minds. While we must always remember that it is our responsibility to proclaim salvation, we must never forget that it is God who saves. It is God who brings men and women under the sound of the gospel, and it is God who brings them to faith in Christ. Our evangelistic work is the instrument that He uses for this purpose, but the power that saves is not in the instrument : it is in the hand of the One who uses the instrument. We must not at any stage forget that. For if we forget that it is God's prerogative to give results when the gospel is preached, we shall start to think that it is our responsibility to secure them. And if we forget that only God can give faith, we shall start to think that the making of converts depends, in the last analysis, not on God, but on us, and that the decisive factor is the way in which we evangelize. And this line of thought, consistently followed through, will lead us far astray.

Let us work this out. If we regarded it as our job, not simply to present Christ, but actually to produce converts—to evangelize, not only faithfully, but also successfully—our approach to evangelism would become pragmatic and calculating. We should conclude that our basic equipment, both for personal dealing and for public preaching, must be twofold. We must have, not merely a clear grasp of the meaning and application of the gospel, but also an irresistible technique for inducing a response. We should, therefore, make it our business to try and develop such a technique. And we should evaluate all evangelism, our own and other people's, by the criterion, not only of the message preached, but also of visible results. If our own efforts were not bearing fruit, we should conclude that our technique still needed improving. If they were bearing fruit, we should conclude that this justified the technique we had been using. We should regard evangelism as an activity involving a battle of wills between ourselves and those to whom we go, a battle in which victory depends on our firing off a heavy enough barrage of calculated effects. Thus our philosophy of evangelism would become terrifyingly similar to the philosophy of brainwashing. And we would no longer be able to argue, when such a similarity is asserted to be a fact, that this is not a proper conception of evangelism.[8] For it *would be* a proper conception of evangelism, if the production of converts was really our responsibility.

This shows us the danger of forgetting the practical implications of God's sovereignty. It is right to recognize our responsibility to engage in aggressive evangelism. It is right to desire the conversion of unbelievers. It is right to want one's presentation of

---

[8] As D. M. Lloyd-Jones argues, in *Conversions: Psychological and Spiritual* (I.V.F., 1959), against the thesis of Dr William Sargant.

the gospel to be as clear and forcible as possible. If we preferred that converts should be few and far between, and did not care whether our proclaiming of Christ went home or not, there would be something wrong with us. But it is not right when we take it on us to do more than God has given us to do. It is not right when we regard ourselves as responsible for securing converts, and look to our own enterprise and techniques to accomplish what only God can accomplish. To do that is to intrude ourselves into the office of the Holy Ghost, and to exalt ourselves as the agents of the new birth. And the point that we must see is this: *only by letting our knowledge of God's sovereignty control the way in which we plan, and pray, and work in His service, can we avoid becoming guilty of this fault.* For where we are not consciously relying on God, there we shall inevitably be found relying on ourselves. And the spirit of self-reliance is a blight on evangelism. Such, however, is the inevitable consequence of forgetting God's sovereignty in the conversion of souls.

But there is an opposite temptation that threatens us also: namely, the temptation to *an exclusive concern with divine sovereignty.*

There are some Christians whose minds are constantly taken up with thoughts of the sovereignty of God. This truth means a great deal to them. It has come to them quite suddenly, perhaps, and with the force of a tremendous revelation. They would say that it has caused a real Copernican revolution in their outlook; it has given a new centre to their entire personal universe. Previously, as they now see,

man had been central in their universe, and God had
been on the circumference. They had thought of
Him as a Spectator of events in His world, rather
than as their Author. They had assumed that the
controlling factor in every situation was man's
handling of it rather than God's plan for it, and they
had looked upon the happiness of human beings as
the most interesting and important thing in creation,
for God no less than for themselves. But now they
see that this man-centred outlook was sinful and
unbiblical; they see that, from one standpoint, the
whole purpose of the Bible is to overthrow it, and
that books like Deuteronomy and Isaiah and John's
Gospel and Romans smash it to smithereens in
almost every chapter; and they realize that henceforth God must be central in their thoughts and
concerns, just as He is central in reality in His own
world. Now they feel the force of the famous first
answer in the Westminster *Shorter Catechism* :
'Man's chief end is to glorify God, and (by so
doing, and in so doing,) to enjoy him for ever.'
Now they see that the way to find the happiness
that God promises is not to seek it as an end in
itself, but to forget oneself in the daily preoccupa-
tion of seeking God's glory and doing His will
and proving His power through the ups and downs
and stresses and strains of everyday life. They see
that it is the glory and praise of God that must
absorb them henceforth, for time and for eternity.
They see that the whole purpose of their existence is
that with heart and life they should worship and
exalt God. In every situation, therefore, their one

question is : what will make most for God's glory?
what should I do in order that in these circumstances
God may be magnified?

And they see, as they ask this question, that,
though God uses men as means for achieving His
purposes, in the last analysis nothing depends on
man; everything depends, rather, on the God who
raises men up to do His will. They see, too, that God
is handling every situation before His servants come
on the scene, and that He continues to handle it and
work out His will in it through each thing that they
do—through their mistakes and failures, no less than
through their personal successes. They see, therefore, that they need never fear for the ark of God,
as Uzzah feared for it, for God will maintain His
own cause. They see that they need never make
Uzzah's mistake, of taking too much on them, and
doing God's work in a forbidden way for fear that
otherwise it would not get done at all.[9] They see
that, since God is always in control, they need never
fear that they will expose Him to loss and damage
if they limit themselves to serving Him in the way
that He has appointed. They see that any other
supposition would in effect be a denial of His wisdom, or His sovereignty, or both. They see, also, that
the Christian must never for one moment imagine
himself to be indispensable to God, or allow himself
to behave as if he were. The God who sent him, and
is pleased to work with him, can do without him.
He must be ready to spend and be spent in the tasks
that God sets him; but he must never suppose that

92 Sa. vi.6 f. Uzzah transgressed the prohibition of Nu. iv.15.

the loss to the Church would be irreparable if God should lay him aside and use someone else. He must not at any point say to himself, 'God's cause would collapse without me and the work I am doing'—for there is never any reason to think this is so. It is never true that God would be at a loss without you and me. Those who have begun to understand the sovereignty of God see all this, and so they seek to efface themselves in all their work for God. They thus bear a practical witness to their belief that God is great, and reigns, by trying to make themselves small, and to act in a way which is itself an acknowledgment that the fruitfulness of their Christian service depends wholly on God, and not upon themselves. And up to this point they are right.

They are, however, beset by exactly the opposite temptation to that discussed above. In their zeal to glorify God by acknowledging His sovereignty in grace, and by refusing to imagine that their own services are indispensable to Him, they are tempted to lose sight of the Church's responsibility to evangelize. Their temptation is to reason thus: 'Agreed, the world is ungodly; but, surely, the less we do about it, the more God will be glorified when at length He breaks in to restore the situation. The most important thing for us to do is to take care that we leave the initiative in His hands.' They are tempted, therefore, to suspect all enterprise in evangelism, whether organized or on the personal level, as if there were something essentially and inescapably man-exalting about it. They are haunted by the fear of running ahead of God, and feel that there is nothing more urgent than to guard against the possibility of doing this.

Perhaps the classic instance of this way of thinking was provided two centuries ago by the chairman of the ministers' fraternal at which William Carey mooted the founding of a missionary society. 'Sit down, young man,' said the old warrior; 'when God is pleased to convert the heathen, He will do it without your aid, or mine!' The idea of taking the initiative in going out to find men of all nations for Christ struck him as improper and, indeed, presumptuous.

Now, think twice before you condemn that old man. He was not entirely without understanding. He had at least grasped that it is God who saves, and that He saves according to His own purpose, and does not take orders from man in the matter. He had grasped too that we must never suppose that without our help God would be helpless. He had, in other words, learned to take the sovereignty of God perfectly seriously. His mistake was that he was not taking the Church's evangelistic responsibility with equal seriousness. He was forgetting that God's way of saving men is to send out His servants to tell them the gospel, and that the Church has been charged to go into all the world for that very purpose.

But this is something that we must not forget. Christ's command means that we all should be devoting all our resources of ingenuity and enterprise to the task of making the gospel known in every possible way to every possible person. Unconcern and inaction with regard to evangelism are always,

therefore, inexcusable. And the doctrine of divine
sovereignty would be grossly misapplied if we should
invoke it in such a way as to lessen the urgency, and
immediacy, and priority, and binding constraint, of
the evangelistic imperative. No revealed truth may
be invoked to extenuate sin. God did not teach us
the reality of His rule in order to give us an excuse
for neglecting His orders.

In our Lord's parable of the talents,[1] the 'good
and faithful' servants were those who furthered their
master's interests by making the most enterprising
lawful use that they could of what was entrusted to
them. The servant who buried his talent, and did
nothing with it beyond keeping it intact, no doubt
imagined that he was being extremely good and
faithful, but his master judged him to be 'wicked',
'slothful', and 'unprofitable'. For what Christ has
given us to use must be put to use; it is not enough
simply to hide it away. We may apply this to our
stewardship of the gospel. The truth about salvation
has been made known to us, not for us simply to
preserve (though we must certainly do that), but
also, and primarily, for us to spread. The light is not
meant to be hidden under the bushel. It is meant to
shine; and it is our business to see that it shines.
'Ye are the light of the world . . .' says our Lord.[2]
He who does not devote himself to evangelism in
every way that he can is not, therefore, playing the
part of a good and faithful servant of Jesus Christ.

Here, then, are two opposite pitfalls: a Scylla
and Charybdis of error. Each is the result of partial

[1] Mt. xxv.14–30.   [2] Mt. v.14–16.

vision, which means partial blindness; each reveals
a failure to face squarely the biblical antinomy of
the responsibility of man and the sovereignty of God.
Both unite to warn us not to pit these truths against
each other, nor to allow either to obscure or over-
shadow the other in our minds. Both unite to warn
us also against reacting from one extreme of error
into the other. If we did that, our last state might
well be worse than the first. What are we to do,
then? To direct our course along the narrow channel
that leads between Scylla and Charybdis; in other
words, to avoid both extremes. How? By making it
our business to believe both these doctrines with all
our might, and to keep both constantly before us for
the guidance and government of our lives.

We shall proceed now according to this maxim.
In what follows, we shall try to take both doctrines
perfectly seriously, as the Bible does, and to view
them in their positive biblical relationship. We shall
not oppose them to each other, for the Bible does
not oppose them to each other. Nor shall we qualify,
or modify, or water down, either of them in terms
of the other, for this is not what the Bible does
either. What the Bible does is to assert both truths
side by side in the strongest and most unambiguous
terms as two ultimate facts; this, therefore, is the
position that we must take in our own thinking.
C. H. Spurgeon was once asked if he could reconcile
these two truths to each other. 'I wouldn't try,' he
replied; 'I never reconcile friends.' Friends?—yes,
friends. This is the point that we have to grasp. In
the Bible, divine sovereignty and human responsi-

bility are not enemies. They are not uneasy neighbours; they are not in an endless state of cold war with each other. They are *friends*, and they work together. I hope that what I am to say now about evangelism will help to make this clear.

CHAPTER III

EVANGELISM

W E shall now try to answer from Scripture the following four questions concerning the Christian's evangelistic responsibility. What is evangelism? What is the evangelistic message? What is the motive for evangelizing? By what means and methods should evangelism be practised?

I. WHAT IS EVANGELISM?

It might be expected that evangelical Christians would not need to spend time discussing this question. In view of the emphasis that Evangelicals always, and rightly, lay on the primacy of evangelism, it would be natural to assume that we were all perfectly unanimous as to what evangelism is. Yet in fact much of the confusion in present-day debates about evangelism arises from lack of agreement at this point. The root of the confusion can be stated in a sentence. It is our widespread and persistent habit of defining evangelism in terms, not of a message delivered, but of an effect produced in our hearers.

For illustration of this, look at the famous definition of evangelism which the Archbishops' Committee gave in its report on the evangelistic work of the Church in 1918. 'To *evangelise*', declared the Committee, 'is *so to present Christ Jesus in the power*

*of the Holy Spirit, that men shall come to put their
trust in God through Him, to accept Him as their
Saviour, and serve Him as their King in the fellowship of His Church.'*

Now this is in many ways an excellent definition.
It states admirably the aim and purpose of the evangelistic enterprise, and rules out many inadequate
and misleading ideas. To start with, it makes the
point that evangelizing means *declaring a specific
message.* According to this definition, it is not evangelism merely to teach general truths about God's
existence, or the moral law; evangelism means *to
present Christ Jesus,* the divine Son who became
man at a particular point in world-history in order
to save a ruined race. Nor, according to this definition, is it evangelism merely to present the teaching
and example of the historical Jesus, or even the truth
about His saving work; evangelism means *to present
Christ Jesus* Himself, the living Saviour and the
reigning Lord. Nor, again, is it evangelism, according to this definition, merely to set forth the living
Jesus as Helper and Friend, without reference to
His saving work on the cross; evangelism means *to
present* Jesus as *Christ,* God's anointed Servant, fulfilling the tasks of His appointed office as Priest and
King. 'The man Christ Jesus' is to be presented as
the 'one mediator between God and men',[1] who
'suffered for sins . . . that he might bring us to God',[2]
the One *through whom,* and through whom alone,
men may *come to put their trust in God,* according
to His own claim : 'I am the way, the truth, and the

[1] 1 Tim. ii.5.   [2] 1 Pet. iii.18.

life : no man cometh unto the Father, but by me.'[3]
He is to be proclaimed as the *Saviour*, the One who
'came into the world to save sinners'[4] and 'redeemed
us from the curse of the law, being made a curse for
us'[5]—'Jesus, which delivereth us from the wrath to
come.'[6] And He is to be set forth as *King* : 'for to
this end Christ died, and lived again, that he might
be Lord of both the dead and the living'.[7] There is
no evangelism where this specific message is not
declared.

Again, the definition makes the point that evangelizing means declaring this specific message *with
a specific application*. It is not evangelism, according
to this definition, to present Christ Jesus as a subject
for detached critical and comparative study. Evangelism, according to this definition, means presenting Christ Jesus and His work in relation to the needs
of fallen men and women, who are without God as
a Father and under the wrath of God as a Judge.
Evangelism means presenting Christ Jesus to them
as their only hope, in this world or the next. Evangelism means exhorting sinners to *accept* Christ
Jesus *as their Saviour*, recognizing that in the most
final and far-reaching sense they are lost without
Him. Nor is this all. Evangelism also means summoning men to receive Christ Jesus as all that He is
—Lord, as well as Saviour—and therefore to *serve
Him as their King in the fellowship of His Church*,
the company of those who worship Him, witness
to Him, and work for Him here on earth. In other

[3] Jn. xiv.6.   [4] 1 Tim. i.15.   [5] Gal. iii.13.
[6] 1 Thes. i.10, RV.   [7] Rom. xiv.9, RV.

words, evangelism is the issuing of a call to turn, as
well as to trust; it is the delivering, not merely of a
divine invitation to receive a Saviour, but of a divine
command to repent of sin. And there is no evangelism where this specific application is not made.

The definition under review establishes these vital
points well. But on one fundamental matter it goes
astray. It puts a consecutive clause where a final
clause should be. Had it begun: 'to evangelise is
to present Christ Jesus to sinful men *in order that*,
through the power of the Holy Spirit, they *may*
come . . .', there would be no fault to find with it.
But it does not say this. What it does say is quite
different. 'To evangelise is *so* to present Christ Jesus
in the power of the Holy Spirit, *that* men *shall*
come . . .' This is to define evangelism in terms of an
effect achieved in the lives of others; which amounts
to saying that the essence of evangelizing is pro-
ducing converts.

But this cannot be right, as we pointed out at an
earlier stage. Evangelism is man's work, but the
giving of faith is God's. It is true, indeed, that every
evangelist's aim is to convert, and that our definition
perfectly expresses the ideal which he longs to see
fulfilled in his own ministry; but the question
whether or not one is evangelizing cannot be settled
simply by asking whether one has had conversions.
There have been missionaries to Moslems who
laboured for a lifetime and saw no converts; must
we conclude from this that they were not evangelizing? There have been un-evangelical preachers
through whose words (not always understood in the

sense intended) individuals have been soundly converted; must we conclude from this that these
preachers were evangelizing after all? The answer,
surely, is no in both cases. The results of preaching
depend, not on the wishes and intentions of men,
but on the will of God Almighty. This consideration
does not mean that we should be indifferent as to
whether we see fruit from our witness to Christ or
not; if fruit is not appearing, we should seek God's
face about it to find out why. But this consideration
does mean that we ought not to define evangelism
in terms of achieved results.

How, then, should evangelism be defined? The
New Testament answer is very simple. According
to the New Testament, evangelism is just preaching
the gospel, the evangel. It is a work of communication in which Christians make themselves mouth-
pieces for God's message of mercy to sinners.
Anyone who faithfully delivers that message, under
whatever circumstances, in a large meeting, in a
small meeting, from a pulpit, or in a private conversation, is evangelizing. Since the divine message
finds its climax in a plea from the Creator to a rebel
world to turn and put faith in Christ, the delivering
of it involves the summoning of one's hearers to
conversion. If you are not, in this sense, seeking to
bring about conversions, you are not evangelizing;
this we have seen already. But the way to tell
whether in fact you are evangelizing is not to ask
whether conversions are known to have resulted
from your witness. It is to ask whether you are
faithfully making known the gospel message.

For a complete picture of what the New Testament means by evangelism, we need not look further than the apostle Paul's account of the nature of his own evangelistic ministry. There are three points to note about it.

1. *Paul evangelized as the commissioned representative of the Lord Jesus Christ.* Evangelism was a task that had been specifically entrusted to him. 'Christ sent me . . . to preach the gospel.'[8] Now, see how he regarded himself in virtue of this commission. In the first place, he saw himself as Christ's *steward*. 'Let a man so account of us (myself, and my fellow-preacher Apollos),' he wrote to the Corinthians, 'as of ministers of Christ, and (in that capacity) stewards of the mysteries of God.'[9] 'A dispensation of the gospel (*i.e.*, a commission to dispense it : "a stewardship", RV) is committed unto me.'[1] Paul saw himself as a bondslave raised to a position of high trust, as the steward of a household in New Testament times always was; he had been 'approved of God to be intrusted with the gospel',[2] and the responsibility now rested on him to be faithful to his trust, as a steward must be,[3] guarding the precious truth that had been committed to him (as he later charges Timothy to do[4]), and distributing and dispensing it according to his Master's instructions. The fact that he had been entrusted with this stewardship meant, as he told the Corinthians, that 'necessity is laid upon me; yea, woe is unto me, if I preach not the

---

[8] 1 Cor. i.17.   [9] 1 Cor. iv.1, RV.   [1] 1 Cor. ix.17.
[2] 1 Thes. ii.4, RV; *cf.* 1 Tim. i.11 f.; Tit. i.3.
[3] *Cf.* 1 Cor. iv.2.   [4] 1 Tim. vi.20; 2 Tim. i.13 f.

gospel!'[5] The figure of stewardship thus highlights Paul's *responsibility* to evangelize.

Again, Paul saw himself as Christ's *herald*. When he describes himself as 'appointed a preacher' of the gospel,[6] the noun he uses is *kēryx*, which means a herald, a person who makes public announcements on another's behalf. When he declares, 'we preach Christ crucified',[7] the verb he uses is *kēryssō*, which denotes the herald's appointed activity of blazoning abroad what he has been told to make known. When Paul speaks of 'my *preaching*', and 'our *preaching*', and lays it down that, after the world's wisdom had rendered the world ignorant of God, 'it pleased God by the foolishness of *preaching* to save them that believe',[8] the noun he uses is *kērygma*, meaning, not the activity of announcing, but the thing announced, the proclamation itself, the message declared. Paul, in his own estimation, was not a philosopher, not a moralist, not one of the world's wise men, but simply Christ's herald. His royal Master had given him a message to proclaim; his whole business, therefore, was to deliver that message with exact and studious faithfulness, adding nothing, altering nothing, and omitting nothing. And he was to deliver it, not as another of man's bright ideas, needing to be beautified with the cosmetics and high heels of fashionable learning in order to make people look at it, but as a word from God, spoken in Christ's name, carrying Christ's authority, and to be authenticated in the

[5] I Cor. ix.16; *cf.* Acts xx.20, 26 f.; 2 Cor. v.10 f.; Ezk. iii.16 ff., xxxiii.7 ff. [6] 2 Tim. i.11; I Tim. ii.7, RV mg.
[7] I Cor. i.23. [8] I Cor. ii.4, xv.14, i.21.

hearers by the convincing power of Christ's Spirit.
'When I came to you,' Paul reminds the Corinthians,
'I . . . came . . . declaring unto you the testimony of
God.' I came, Paul is saying, not to give you my own
ideas about anything, but simply to deliver God's
message. Therefore, 'I determined not to know any
thing among you, save Jesus Christ, and him crucified'—for it was just this that God sent me to tell
you about. 'And my speech and my preaching
(*kērygma*) was not with enticing words of man's
wisdom, but in demonstration of the Spirit and of
power; that your faith should not stand in the wisdom of men, but in the power of God.'[9] The figure
of the herald thus highlights the *authenticity* of
Paul's gospel.

Thirdly, Paul considered himself Christ's *ambassador*. What is an ambassador? He is the authorized
representative of a sovereign. He speaks, not in his
own name, but on behalf of the ruler whose deputy
he is, and his whole duty and responsibility is to
interpret that ruler's mind faithfully to those to
whom he is sent. Paul used this figure twice, both
times in connection with his evangelistic work. Pray
for me, he wrote from prison, 'that I may open my
mouth boldly, to make known the mystery of the
gospel, for which I am an *ambassador* in bonds: that
therein I may speak boldly, as I ought to speak.'
God, he wrote again, has 'committed unto us the
word of reconciliation. We are *ambassadors* therefore on behalf of Christ, as though God were intreat-

[9] I Cor. ii.1–5. The argument is not affected if for 'testimony' we read 'mystery' in verse 1, as RV does.

ing by us : we beseech you on behalf of Christ, be ye reconciled to God.'[1] Paul called himself an ambassador because he knew that, when he proclaimed the gospel facts and promises, and urged sinners to receive the reconciliation effected at Calvary, it was Christ's message to the world that he was declaring. The figure of ambassadorship thus highlights the *authority* that Paul had, as representing his Lord.

In his evangelism, then, Paul consciously acted as the slave and steward, the mouthpiece and herald, the spokesman and ambassador, of the Lord Jesus Christ. Hence, on the one hand, his sustained boldness and unshakable sense of authority in face of ridicule and indifference; hence, on the other hand, his intransigent refusal to modify his message in order to suit circumstances. These two things, of course, were connected, for Paul could regard himself as speaking with Christ's authority only as long as he remained faithful to the terms of his commission and said neither less nor more than he had been given to say.[2] But while he preached the gospel that Christ had entrusted to him, he spoke as Christ's commissioned representative, and could therefore speak authoritatively, and claim a right to be heard.

But the commission to publish the gospel and make disciples was never confined to the apostles. Nor is it now confined to the Church's ministers. It is a commission that rests upon the whole Church collectively, and therefore upon each Christian individually. All God's people are sent to do as the

---

[1] Eph. vi. 19 f.; 2 Cor. v. 19 f., RV.   [2] *Cf*. Gal. i. 8 ff.

Philippians did, and 'shine as lights in the world; holding forth the word of life'.[3] Every Christian, therefore, has a God-given obligation to make known the gospel of Christ. And every Christian who declares the gospel message to any fellow-man does so as Christ's ambassador and representative, according to the terms of his God-given commission. Such is the authority, and such the responsibility, of the Church and of the Christian in evangelism.

2. The second point in Paul's understanding of his own evangelistic ministry follows on from the first. *His primary task in evangelism was to teach the truth about the Lord Jesus Christ.*

As Christ's ambassador, Paul's first job was to 'get acrosss' the message that his Sovereign had charged him to deliver. Christ sent me, he declared, —to do what?—'to preach the gospel'.[4] The Greek word here is *euangelizomai*, meaning publish the *euangelion*, literally the 'good news'. For that is what Paul's gospel was. Good news, Paul proclaimed, has come into the world—good news from God. It is unlike anything that the world, Jewish or Gentile, had guessed or expected, but it is something that the whole world needs. This good news, the 'word of God' in the usual New Testament sense of that phrase,[5] 'the truth' as Paul often calls it,[6] is a full and final disclosure of what the Creator has done, and will do, to save sinners. It is a complete unfold-

[3] Phil. ii.15 f.   [4] 1 Cor. i.17.
[5] *Cf.* Acts iv.31, viii.14, xi.1, xiii.46; 2 Cor. ii.17; Col. i.25; 1 Thes. ii.13; 2 Tim. ii.9.
[6] *Cf.* 2 Cor. iv.2; Gal. ii.5, 14; 2 Thes. ii.10 ff.; 2 Tim. ii.18, 25, iii.8.

ing of the spiritual facts of life in God's apostate
world.

What was this good news that Paul preached?
It was the news about Jesus of Nazareth. It was the
news of the incarnation, the atonement, and the
kingdom—the cradle, the cross, and the crown—of
the Son of God. It was the news of how God 'glorified his servant Jesus'[7] by making Him Christ, the
world's long-awaited 'Prince and . . . Saviour'.[8] It
was the news of how God made His Son Man; and
how, as Man, God made Him Priest, and Prophet,
and King; and how, as Priest, God also made Him
a sacrifice for sins; and how, as Prophet, God also
made Him a Lawgiver to His people; and how, as
King, God has also made Him Judge of all the
world, and given Him prerogatives which in the
Old Testament are exclusively Jehovah's own—
namely, to reign till every knee bows before Him,
and to save all who call on His name. In short, the
good news was just this : that God has executed His
eternal intention of glorifying His Son by exalting
Him as a great Saviour for great sinners.

Such was the gospel which Paul was sent to
preach. It was a message of some complexity, needing to be learned before it could be lived by, and
understood before it could be applied. It needed,
therefore, to be *taught*. Hence Paul, as a preacher
of it, had to become a teacher. He saw this as part
of his calling; he speaks of 'the gospel : whereunto
I am appointed a preacher . . . *and a teacher*'.[9]

[7] Acts iii.13, RV.   [8] Acts v.31.   [9] 2 Tim. i.10 f.

And he tells us that teaching was basic to his evangelistic practice; he speaks of 'Christ . . . whom we preach . . . *teaching every man* in all wisdom'.[1] In both texts the reference to teaching is explanatory of the reference to preaching. In other words: it is by teaching that the gospel preacher fulfils his ministry. To *teach* the gospel is his first responsibility: to reduce it to its simplest essentials, to analyse it point by point, to fix its meaning by positive and negative definition, to show how each part of the message links up with the rest—and to go on explaining it till he is quite sure that his listeners have grasped it. And therefore when Paul preached the gospel, formally or informally, in the synagogue or in the streets, to Jews or to Gentiles, to a crowd or to one man, what he did was to *teach* —engaging attention, capturing interest, setting out the facts, explaining their significance, solving difficulties, answering objections, and showing how the message bears on life. Luke's regular way of describing Paul's evangelistic ministry is to say that he *disputed*,[2] or *reasoned* (*dialegomai*: RSV renders 'argued'),[3] or *taught*,[4] or *persuaded* (*i.e.*, sought to carry his hearers' judgments).[5] And Paul himself refers to his ministry among the Gentiles as primarily a task of instruction: 'unto me . . . was this grace given, to preach unto the Gentiles the unsearchable riches of Christ; and *to make all men see* what is the

[1] Col. i.28.   [2] Acts ix.29.
[3] Acts xvii.2, 17, RV, xviii.4, xix.8 f., RV, xxiv.25.
[4] Acts xviii.11, xxviii.31.
[5] Acts xviii.4, xix.8, 26, xxviii.23; *cf.* xxvi.28.

dispensation of the mystery . . .'[6] Clearly, in Paul's view, his first and fundamental job as a preacher of the gospel was to communicate knowledge—to get gospel truth fixed in men's minds. To him, teaching the truth was the basic evangelistic activity; to him, therefore, the only right method of evangelism was the teaching method.

3. *Paul's ultimate aim in evangelism was to convert his hearers to faith in Christ.*

The word 'convert' is a translation of the Greek *epistrephō*, which means—and is sometimes translated—'turn'. We think of conversion as a work of God, and so from one standpoint it is; but it is striking to observe that in the three New Testament passages where *epistrephō* is used transitively, of 'converting' someone to God, the subject of the verb is not God, as we might have expected, but a preacher. The angel said of John the Baptist : 'Many of the children of Israel shall he *turn* to the Lord their God.'[7] James says : 'Brethren, if any of you do err from the truth, and one *convert* him; let him know, that he which *converteth* the sinner . . . shall save a soul from death . . .'[8] And Paul himself tells Agrippa how Christ had said to him : 'I send thee (to the Gentiles) to open their eyes, and to *turn* them from darkness to light, and from the power of Satan unto God', and how he had obeyed the heavenly vision by proclaiming to both Jews and Gentiles 'that they should repent and *turn* to God'.[9] These passages represent the converting of others as the

[6] Eph. iii.8, RV.   [7] Lk. i.16.   [8] Jas. v.19 f.
[9] Acts xxvi. 17 ff.

work of God's people, a task which they are to perform by summoning men to turn to God in repentance and faith.

When the Scriptures speak in this way of converting, and of saving, too, as a task for God's people to
perform, they are not, of course, calling in question
the truth that, properly speaking, it is God who
converts and saves. What they are saying is simply
that the conversion and salvation of others should
be the Christian's objective. The preacher should
work to convert his congregation; the wife should
work to save her unbelieving husband.[1] Christians
are sent to convert, and they should not allow themselves, as Christ's representatives in the world, to
aim at anything less. Evangelizing, therefore, is not
simply a matter of teaching, and instructing, and
imparting information to the mind. There is more
to it than that. Evangelizing includes the endeavour
to elicit a response to the truth taught. It is communication with a view to conversion. It is a matter,
not merely of informing, but also of inviting. It is
an attempt to *gain*, or *win*, or *catch*, our fellow-men
for Christ.[2] Our Lord depicts it as fishermen's work.[3]

Paul, again, is our model here. Paul, as we saw,
knew himself to be sent by Christ, not only to open
men's minds by teaching them the gospel (though
that must come first), but also to turn them to God
by exhorting, and applying the truth to their lives.
Accordingly, his avowed aim was not just to spread
information, but to save sinners : 'that I may by all

---

[1] I Cor. vii.16.   [2] See I Cor. ix.19 ff.; I Pet. iii.1; Lk. v.10.
                       [3] Mt. iv.19; *cf.* xiii.47.

means save some'.[4] Thus, there was in his evangelistic preaching both instruction—'God was in Christ
reconciling the world unto himself'—and entreaty
—'we beseech you on behalf of Christ, be ye reconciled to God'.[5] His responsibility extended, not only
towards the gospel which he was charged to preach
and preserve, but also towards the needy people to
whom he was sent to impart it, and who were perishing without it.[6] As an apostle of Christ, he was more
than a teacher of truth; he was a shepherd of souls,
sent into the world, not to lecture sinners, but to love
them. For he was an apostle second, and a Christian
first; and, as a Christian, he was a man called to love
his neighbour. This meant simply that in every
situation, and by every means in his power, it was
his business to seek other people's good. From this
standpoint, the significance of his apostolic commission to evangelize and found churches was simply
that this was the particular way in which Christ was
calling him to fulfil the law of love to his neighbour.
He might not, therefore, preach the gospel in a
harsh, callous way, putting it before his neighbour
with a contemptuous air of 'there you are—take it
or leave it', and excusing himself for his unconcern
about people on the grounds of his faithfulness to
the truth. Such conduct would be a failure of love
on his part. His business was to present truth in a
spirit of love, as an expression and implementation
of his desire to save his hearers. The attitude which
informed all Paul's evangelism was this: 'I seek not

[4] 1 Cor. ix.22, RV; cf. Rom. xi.14.   [5] 2 Cor. v.19 f., RV.
[6] Cf. Rom. i.13 ff.

yours, but you . . . and I will very gladly spend and be spent for you.'[7]

And all our own evangelism must be done in the same spirit. As love to our neighbour suggests and demands that we evangelize, so the command to evangelize is a specific application of the command to love others for Christ's sake, and must be fulfilled as such.

Love made Paul warm-hearted and affectionate in his evangelism. 'We were gentle among you,' he reminded the Thessalonians; 'being affectionately desirous of you, we were willing to have imparted unto you, not the gospel of God only, but also our own souls, because ye were dear unto us.'[8] Love also made Paul considerate and adaptable in his evangelism; though he peremptorily refused to change his message to please men,[9] he would go to any lengths in his presentation of it to avoid giving offence, and putting needless difficulties in the way of men's accepting and responding to it. 'Though I was free from all men,' he wrote to the Corinthians, 'I brought myself under bondage to all, that I might gain the more. And to the Jews I became as a Jew, that I might gain Jews; to them that are under the law, as under the law . . . that I might gain them that are under the law; to them that are without law, as without law . . . that I might gain them that are without law. To the weak I became weak, that I might gain the weak; I am become all things to all men, that I may by all means save

---

[7] 2 Cor. xii.14 f.   [8] 1 Thes. ii.7 f.
[9] Cf. Gal. i.10; 2 Cor. ii.17; 1 Thes. ii.4.

some.'[1] Paul sought to save men; and because he sought to save them, he was not content merely to throw truth at them; but he went out of his way to get alongside them, and to start thinking with them from where they were, and to speak to them in terms that they could understand, and above all to avoid everything that would prejudice them against the gospel, and so put stumbling-blocks in their path. In his zeal to maintain truth he never lost sight of the needs and claims of people. His aim and object in all his handling of the gospel, even in the heat of the polemics which contrary views evoked, was never less than to win souls, by converting those whom he saw as his neighbours to faith in the Lord Jesus Christ.

Such was evangelism according to Paul: going out in love, as Christ's agent in the world, to teach sinners the truth of the gospel with a view to converting and saving them. If, therefore, we are engaging in this activity, in this spirit, and with this aim, we are evangelizing, irrespective of the particular means by which we are doing it.

We saw earlier how wrong our thinking would go if we defined evangelism too broadly, and fell into assuming that the production of converts was our personal responsibility. We would now point out that there is an opposite mistake which we must also avoid: the mistake, that is, of defining evangelism too narrowly. One way of making this mistake

[1] I Cor. ix.19 ff., RV; *cf.* x.33.

would be to define evangelism institutionally, in terms of holding some particular type of evangelistic meeting—a meeting, let us say, run on informal lines, at which testimonies are given, choruses are sung, and an appeal is made at the close for some outward sign of having received Christ, such as raising the hand, or standing, or walking to the front. Should we equate the Church's evangelistic responsibility with the holding of such meetings, or the Christian's evangelistic responsibility with bringing unconverted people to such meetings, we should be grievously astray, as the following considerations will show.

1. In the first place, there are many ways of bringing the gospel before the unconverted in order to win them, besides getting them to meetings of this type. There is, to start with, the way of personal evangelism, by which Andrew won Peter, and Philip won Nathanael, and Paul won Onesimus.[2] There is the home meeting, and the group Bible study. Also, and most important, there are the regular services Sunday by Sunday in local churches. Insofar as the preaching at our Sunday services is scriptural, those services will of necessity be evangelistic. It is a mistake to suppose that evangelistic sermons are a special brand of sermons, having their own peculiar style and conventions; evangelistic sermons are just scriptural sermons, the sort of sermons that a man cannot help preaching if he is preaching the Bible biblically. Proper sermons seek to expound and apply what is in the Bible. But what is in the Bible

[2] Jn. i.40 ff., 43 ff.; Phm.10

is just the whole counsel of God for man's salvation; all Scripture bears witness, in one way or another, to Christ, and all biblical themes relate to Him. All proper sermons, therefore, will of necessity declare Christ in some fashion, and so be more or less directly evangelistic. Some sermons, of course, will aim more narrowly and exclusively at converting sinners than do others. But you cannot present the Lord Jesus Christ as the Bible presents Him, as God's answer to every problem in the sinner's relationship with Himself, and not be in effect evangelistic all the time. The Lord Jesus Christ, said Robert Bolton, is 'offered most freely, and without exception of any person, every Sabbath, every Sermon, either in plaine, and direct terms, or implyedly, at the least.'[3] So it is, inevitably, wherever the Bible is preached biblically. And there is something terribly wrong in any church, or any man's ministry, to which Bolton's generalization does not apply. If in our churches 'evangelistic' meetings, and 'evangelistic' sermons, are thought of as special occasions, different from the ordinary run of things, it is a damning indictment of our normal Sunday services. So that if we should imagine that the essential work of evangelism lies in holding meetings of the special type described out of church hours, so to speak, that would simply prove that we had failed to understand what our regular Sunday services are for.

2. Secondly, imagine a local church, or fellowship of Christians, who are giving themselves whole-

---

[3] *Instructions for a Right Comforting Afflicted Consciences,* 3rd. ed. (1640), p. 185.

heartedly to evangelism by the means mentioned
above—personal work, home meetings, and gospel
preaching at their ordinary services—but have never
had occasion to hold, or to join in, evangelistic meetings of the special sort that we are considering. If
we equated the Christian duty of evangelism with
running and supporting such meetings, we should
have to conclude that this church or fellowship, because it eschewed them, was not evangelizing at all.
But that would be like arguing that you cannot
really be an Englishman unless you live at Frinton-
on-Sea. And it would surely be a little odd to condemn people for not evangelizing just because they
do not join in meetings of a type of which there is
no trace in the New Testament. Was no evangelizing
done, then, in New Testament times?

3. In the third place, it needs to be said that a
meeting, or service, is not necessarily evangelistic just
because it includes testimonies, and choruses, and an
appeal, any more than a man is necessarily English
because he wears striped trousers and a bowler hat.
The way to find out whether a particular service was
evangelistic is to ask, not whether an appeal for
decision was made, but what truth was taught at it.
If it transpired that insufficient of the gospel was
preached to make the appeal for response intelligible
to the congregation, the right of the meeting to be
called evangelistic would be very doubtful.

We say these things, not to grind a polemical axe,
but simply in the interests of clear thinking. It is no
part of our purpose to belittle evangelistic meetings
and campaigns as such. We are not suggesting that

there is no place at all for special evangelistic meetings; that, in face of the rampant paganism of the modern world, would be excessively foolish. The only point we are making here is that there is a place for other forms of evangelistic action too; indeed, under certain circumstances, a prior place. Because God has used meetings, and series of meetings, of this type in the past, there is a certain surface plausibility about the idea that they constitute the normal and natural, and necessary, and indeed only, pattern of evangelism for the present and the future. But this does not follow. There can be evangelism without these meetings. They are in no way essential to the practice of evangelism. Wherever, and by whatever means, the gospel is communicated with a view to conversion, there you have evangelism. Evangelism is to be defined, not institutionally, in terms of the kind of meeting held, but theologically, in terms of what is taught, and for what purpose.

What principles should guide us in assessing the value of different methods of evangelism, and how much the Christian duty to evangelize really involves for us, we shall discuss at a later stage.

II. WHAT IS THE EVANGELISTIC MESSAGE?

We shall have to deal with this fairly summarily. In a word, the evangelistic message is the gospel of Christ, and Him crucified; the message of man's sin and God's grace, of human guilt and divine forgiveness, of new birth and new life through the gift of the Holy Spirit. It is a message made up of four essential ingredients.

1. The gospel is a message about *God*. It tells us who He is, what His character is, what His standards are, and what He requires of us, His creatures. It tells us that we owe our very existence to Him, that for good or ill we are always in His hands and under His eye, and that He made us to worship and serve Him, to show forth His praise and to live for His glory. These truths are the foundation of theistic religion, and until they are grasped the rest of the gospel message will seem neither cogent nor relevant. It is here, with the assertion of man's complete and constant dependence on his Creator, that the Christian story starts.

We can learn again from Paul at this point. When preaching to Jews, as at Pisidian Antioch,[4] he did not need to mention the fact that men were God's creatures; he could take this knowledge for granted, for his hearers had the Old Testament faith behind them. He could begin at once to declare Christ to them, as the fulfilment of Old Testament hopes. But when preaching to Gentiles, who knew nothing of the Old Testament, Paul had to go further back, and start from the beginning. And the beginning from which Paul started in such cases was the doctrine of God's Creatorship, and man's creaturehood. So, when the Athenians asked him to explain what his talk of Jesus and the resurrection was all about, he spoke to them first of God the Creator, and what He made man for. 'God . . . made the world . . . he giveth to all life, and breath, and all things; and hath made . . . all nations . . . that they should seek

[4] Acts xiii.16 ff.

the Lord.'[5] This was not, as some have supposed, a piece of philosophical apologetic of a kind that Paul afterwards renounced, but the first and basic lesson in theistic faith. The gospel starts by teaching us that we, as creatures, are absolutely dependent on God, and that He, as Creator, has an absolute claim on us. Only when we have learned this can we see what sin is, and only when we see what sin is can we understand the good news of salvation from sin. We must know what it means to call God Creator before we can grasp what it means to speak of Him as Redeemer. Nothing can be achieved by talking about sin and salvation where this preliminary lesson has not in some measure been learned.

2. The gospel is a message about *sin*. It tells us how we have fallen short of God's standard; how we have become guilty, filthy, and helpless in sin, and now stand under the wrath of God. It tells us that the reason why we sin continually is that we are sinners by nature, and that nothing we do, or try to do, for ourselves can put us right, or bring us back into God's favour. It shows us ourselves as God sees us, and teaches us to think of ourselves as God thinks of us. Thus it leads us to self-despair. And this also is a necessary step. Not till we have learned our need to get right with God, and our inability to do so by any effort of our own, can we come to know the Christ who saves from sin.

There is a pitfall here. Everybody's life includes things which cause dissatisfaction and shame. Everyone has a bad conscience about some things in his

[5] Acts xvii.24 ff. See also Acts xiv.15 ff.

past, matters in which he has fallen short of the standard which he set for himself, or which was expected of him by others. The danger is that in our evangelism we should content ourselves with evoking thoughts of these things and making people feel uncomfortable about them, and then depicting Christ as the One who saves us from these elements of ourselves, without even raising the question of our relationship with God. But this is just the question that has to be raised when we speak about sin. For the very idea of sin in the Bible is of an offence against God, which disrupts a man's relationship with God. Unless we see our shortcomings in the light of the law and holiness of God, we do not see them *as sin* at all. For sin is not a social concept; it is a theological concept. Though sin is committed by man, and many sins are against society, sin cannot be defined in terms of either man or society. We never know what sin really is till we have learned to think of it in terms of God, and to measure it, not by human standards, but by the yardstick of His total demand on our lives.

What we have to grasp, then, is that the bad conscience of the natural man is not at all the same thing as conviction of sin. It does not, therefore, follow that a man is convicted of sin when he is distressed about his weaknesses and the wrong things he has done. It is not conviction of sin just to feel miserable about yourself and your failures and your inadequacy to meet life's demands. Nor would it be saving faith if a man in that condition called on the Lord Jesus Christ just to soothe him, and cheer him up, and make him feel confident again. Nor should we be preaching the gospel (though we might imagine we were) if all that we did was to present Christ in terms of a man's felt wants. ('Are you happy? Are you satisfied? Do you want peace of mind? Do you feel that you have failed? Are you fed up with yourself? Do you want a friend? Then come to Christ; He will meet your every need . . .'— as if the Lord Jesus Christ were to be thought of as a fairy godmother, or a super-psychiatrist.) No; we have to go deeper than this. To preach sin means, not to make capital out of people's felt frailties (the brainwasher's trick), but to measure their lives by the holy law of God. To be convicted of sin means, not just to feel that one is an all-round flop, but to realize that one has offended God, and flouted His authority, and defied Him, and gone against Him, and put oneself in the wrong with Him. To preach Christ means to set Him forth as the One who through His cross sets men right with God again. To put faith in Christ means relying on Him, and Him alone, to restore us to God's fellowship and favour.

It is indeed true that the real Christ, the Christ of the Bible, who offers Himself to us as a Saviour from sin and an Advocate with God, does in fact give peace, and joy, and moral strength, and the privilege of His own friendship, to those who trust Him. But the Christ who is depicted and desired merely to make the lot of life's casualties easier by supplying them with aids and comforts is not the real Christ, but a misrepresented and misconceived

Christ—in effect, an imaginary Christ. And if we taught people to look to an imaginary Christ, we should have no grounds for expecting that they would find a real salvation. We must be on our guard, therefore, against equating a natural bad conscience and sense of wretchedness with spiritual conviction of sin, and so omitting in our evangelism to impress upon sinners the basic truth about their condition—namely, that their sin has alienated them from God, and exposed them to His condemnation, and hostility, and wrath, so that their first need is for a restored relationship with Him.

It may be asked: what are the signs of true conviction of sin, as distinct from the mere smart of a natural bad conscience, or the mere disgust at life which any disillusioned person may feel?

The signs seem to be three in number.

(i) Conviction of sin is essentially an awareness of *a wrong relationship with God*: not just with one's neighbour, or one's own conscience and ideals for oneself, but with one's Maker, the God in whose hand one's breath is and on whom one depends for existence every moment. To define conviction of sin as a sense of need, without qualification, would not be enough; it is not any sense of need, but a sense of a particular need—a need, namely, for restoration of fellowship with God. It is the realization that, as one stands at present, one is in a relationship with God that spells only rejection, and retribution, and wrath, and pain, for the present and the future; and a realization that this is an intolerable relationship to remain in, and therefore a desire that, at whatever cost and on whatever terms, it might be changed. Conviction of sin may centre upon the sense of one's guilt before God, or one's uncleanness in His sight, or one's rebellion against Him, or one's alienation and estrangement from Him; but always it is a sense of the need to get right, not simply with oneself or other people, but with God.

(*ii*) Conviction of sin always includes conviction of *sins*: a sense of guilt for particular wrongs done in the sight of God, from which one needs to turn, and be rid of them, if one is ever to be right with God. Thus, Isaiah was convicted specifically of sins of speech,[6] and Zacchaeus of sins of extortion.[7]

(*iii*) Conviction of sin always includes conviction of *sinfulness*: a sense of one's complete corruption and perversity in God's sight, and one's consequent need of what Ezekiel called a 'new heart',[8] and our Lord a new birth,[9] *i.e.* a moral re-creation. Thus, the author of Psalm li—traditionally identified with David, convicted of his sin with Bathsheba—confesses, not only particular transgressions (verses 1–4), but also the depravity of his nature (verses 5–6), and seeks cleansing from the guilt and defilement of both (verses 7–10). Indeed, perhaps the shortest way to tell whether a person is convicted of sin or not is to take him through Psalm li, and see whether his heart is in fact speaking anything like the language of the psalmist.

3. The gospel is a message about *Christ*—Christ the Son of God incarnate; Christ the Lamb of God,

[6] Is. vi.5.   [7] Lk. xix.8.   [8] Ezk. xxxvi.26.   [9] Jn. iii.3 ff.

dying for sin; Christ the risen Lord; Christ the perfect Saviour.

Two points need to be made about the declaring
of this part of the message.

(i) *We must not present the Person of Christ apart
from His saving work.*

It is sometimes said that it is the presentation of
Christ's Person, rather than of doctrines about Him,
that draws sinners to His feet. It is true that it is the
living Christ who saves, and that a theory of the
atonement, however orthodox, is no substitute.
When this remark is made, however, what is usually
being suggested is that doctrinal instruction is dispensable in evangelistic preaching, and that all the
evangelist need do is paint a vivid word-picture of
the Man of Galilee who went about doing good, and
then assure his hearers that this Jesus is still alive
to help them in their troubles. But such a message
could hardly be called the gospel. It would, in
reality, be a mere conundrum, serving only to
mystify. Who was this Jesus? we should ask; and
what is His position now? Such preaching would
raise these questions while concealing the answers.
And thus it would completely baffle the thoughtful
listener.

For the truth is that you cannot make sense of the
historic figure of Jesus till you know about the *incarnation*—that this Jesus was in fact God the Son,
made man to save sinners according to His Father's
eternal purpose. Nor can you make sense of His life
till you know about the *atonement*—that He lived

as man so that He might die as man for men, and that His passion, His judicial murder, was really His saving action of bearing away the world's sins. Nor can you tell on what terms to approach Him now till you know about the *resurrection, ascension,* and *heavenly session*—that Jesus has been raised, and enthroned, and made King, and lives to save to the uttermost all who acknowledge His Lordship. These doctrines, to mention no others, are essential to the gospel. Without them, there is no gospel, only a puzzle story about a man named Jesus. To oppose the teaching of doctrines about Christ to the presenting of His Person is, therefore, to put asunder two things which God has joined. It is really very perverse indeed; for the whole purpose of teaching these doctrines in evangelism is to throw light on the Person of the Lord Jesus Christ, and to make clear to our hearers just who it is that we want them to meet. When, in ordinary social life, we want people to know who it is that we are introducing them to, we tell them something about him, and what he has done; and so it is here. The apostles themselves preached these doctrines in order to preach Christ, as the New Testament shows. In fact, without these doctrines you would have no gospel to preach at all.

(*ii*) But there is a second and complementary point. *We must not present the saving work of Christ apart from His Person.*

Evangelistic preachers and personal workers have sometimes been known to make this mistake. In their concern to focus attention on the atoning death

of Christ, as the sole sufficient ground on which sinners may be accepted with God, they have ex-
pounded the summons to saving faith in these terms:
'Believe that Christ died for your sins.' The effect
of this exposition is to represent the saving work of
Christ in the past, dissociated from His Person in
the present, as the whole object of our trust. But it
is not biblical thus to isolate the work from the
Worker. Nowhere in the New Testament is the call
to believe expressed in such terms. What the New
Testament calls for is faith in (*en*) or into (*eis*) or
upon (*epi*) Christ Himself—the placing of our trust
in the living Saviour, who died for sins. The object
of saving faith is thus not, strictly speaking, the
atonement, but the Lord Jesus Christ, who made
atonement. We must not in presenting the gospel
isolate the cross and its benefits from the Christ
whose cross it was. For the persons to whom the
benefits of Christ's death belong are just those who
trust His Person, and believe, not upon His saving
death simply, but upon *Him*, the living Saviour. 'Believe on *the Lord Jesus Christ*, and thou shalt be
saved,'[1] said Paul. 'Come unto *me* . . . and *I* will
give you rest,'[2] said our Lord.

This being so, one thing becomes clear straight
away : namely, that the question about the extent
of the atonement, which is being much agitated in
some quarters, has no bearing on the content of the
evangelistic message at this particular point. I do
not propose to discuss this question now; I have done

[1] Acts xvi.31.   [2] Mt. xi.28.

that elsewhere.[3] I am not at present asking you whether you think it is true to say that Christ died in order to save every single human being, past, present, and future, or not. Nor am I at present inviting you to make up your mind on this question, if you have not done so already. All I want to say here is that even if you think the above assertion is true, your presentation of Christ in evangelism ought not to differ from that of the man who thinks it false.

What I mean is this. It is obvious that if a preacher thought that the statement, 'Christ died for every one of you', made to any congregation, would be unverifiable, and probably not true, he would take care not to make it in his gospel preaching. You do not find such statements in the sermons of, for instance, George Whitefield or Charles Spurgeon. But now, my point is that, even if a man thinks that this statement would be true if he made it, it is not a thing that he ever needs to say, or ever has reason to say, when preaching the gospel. For preaching the

[3] In my introduction to the 1959 reprint of *The Death of Death in the Death of Christ*, by John Owen. Owen's book is a classical discussion of the complex of questions which the controversy about 'limited atonement' involves. The central issue does not concern the value of the atonement, considered in itself, nor the availability of Christ to those who would trust Him as their Saviour. All agree that no limit can be set to the intrinsic worth of Christ's death, and that Christ never casts out those who come to Him. The cleavage is over the question, whether the intention of the Father and the Son in the great transaction of Calvary was to save any more than actually are saved. There is no room here to open up this elaborate question; and in any case, nothing in the text depends one way or the other on the answer that one gives to it.

gospel, as we have just seen, means inviting sinners
to come to Jesus Christ, the living Saviour, who, by
virtue of His atoning death, is able to forgive and
save all those who put their trust in Him. What has
to be said about the cross when preaching the gospel
is simply that Christ's death is the ground on which
Christ's forgiveness is given. And this is all that has
to be said. The question of the designed extent of
the atonement does not come into the story at all.

The fact is that the New Testament never calls
on any man to repent on the ground that Christ died
specifically and particularly for him. The basis on
which the New Testament invites sinners to put
faith in Christ is simply that they need Him, and
that He offers Himself to them, and that those who
receive Him are promised all the benefits that His
death secured for His people. What is universal and
all-inclusive in the New Testament is the invitation
to faith, and the promise of salvation to all who
believe.[4]

Our task in evangelism is to reproduce as faithfully as possible the New Testament emphasis. To go
beyond the New Testament, or to distort its view-
point or shift its stress, is always wrong. And therefore—if we may at this point speak in the words of
James Denney—'we do not think of separating
(Christ's) work from Him who achieved it. The New
Testament knows only of a living Christ, and all

---

[4] See Mt. xi.28 ff., xxii.9; Lk. ii.10 f., xii.8; Jn. i.12, iii.14
ff., vi.40, 54, vii.37, xi.26, xii.46; Acts ii.21, x.43, xiii.39; Rom.
i.16, iii.22, ix.33, x.4 ff.; Gal. iii.22; Tit. ii.11; Rev. xxii.17;
cf. Is. lv.1.

apostolic preaching of the gospel holds up the living Christ to men. But the living Christ is Christ who died, and He is never preached apart from His death, and from its reconciling power. It is *the living Christ, with the virtue of His reconciling death in Him*, who is the burden of the apostolic message ... The task of the evangelist is to preach *Christ ... in His character as the Crucified.*[5] The gospel is not, 'believe that Christ died for everybody's sins, and therefore for yours,' any more than it is, 'believe that Christ died only for certain people's sins, and so perhaps not for yours.' The gospel is, 'believe on the Lord Jesus Christ, who died for sins, and now offers you Himself as your Saviour.' This is the message which we are to take to the world. We have no business to ask them to put faith in any view of the extent of the atonement; our job is to point them to the living Christ, and summon them to trust in Him.

It was because they had both grasped this that John Wesley and George Whitefield could regard each other as brothers in evangelism, though they differed on the extent of the atonement. For their views on this subject did not enter into their gospel preaching. Both were content to preach the gospel just as it stands in Scripture : that is, to proclaim 'the living Christ, with the virtue of His reconciling death in Him', to offer Him to sinners, and to invite the lost to come to Him and so find life.

4. This brings us to the final ingredient in the

[5] *The Christian Doctrine of Reconciliation*, p. 287; my italics.

gospel message. The gospel is a summons to *faith and repentance*.

All who hear the gospel are summoned by God to repent and believe. 'God . . . commandeth all men every where to *repent*,' Paul told the Athenians.[6] When asked by His hearers what they should do in order to 'work the works of God', our Lord replied : 'This is the work of God, that ye *believe* on him whom he hath sent.'[7] And in 1 John iii.23 we read: 'This is his *commandment*, That we should believe on the name of his Son Jesus Christ . . .' Repentance and faith are rendered matters of duty by God's direct command, and hence impenitence and unbelief are singled out in the New Testament as most grievous sins.[8] With these universal commands, as we indicated above, go universal promises of salvation to all who obey them. 'Through his name *whosoever believeth* in him shall receive remission of sins.'[9] '*Whosoever will*, let him take the water of life freely.'[1] 'God so loved the world, that he gave his only begotten Son, that *whosoever believeth* in him should not perish, but have everlasting life.'[2] These words are promises to which God will stand as long as time shall last.

It needs to be said that faith is not a mere optimistic feeling, any more than repentance is a mere regretful or remorseful feeling. Faith and repentance are both acts, and acts of the whole man. Faith is more than just credence; faith is essentially the

[6] Acts xvii.30.   [7] Jn. vi.29.
[8] *Cf.* Lk. xiii.3, 5; 2 Thes. ii.11 f.   [9] Acts x.43.
                 [1] Rev. xxii.17.   [2] Jn. iii.16.

casting and resting of oneself and one's confidence
on the promises of mercy which Christ has given to
sinners, and on the Christ who gave those promises.
Equally, repentance is more than just sorrow for the
past; repentance is a change of mind and heart, a
new life of denying self and serving the Saviour as
king in self's place. Mere credence without trusting,
and mere remorse without turning, do not save. 'The
devils also believe, and tremble.'[3] 'The sorrow of the
world worketh death.'[4]

Two further points need to be made also.

(i) The demand is for *faith as well as repentance*.
It is not enough to resolve to turn from sin, and give
up evil habits, and try to put Christ's teaching into
practice by being religious and doing all possible
good to others. Aspiration, and resolution, and mor-
ality, and religiosity, are no substitutes for faith.
Martin Luther and John Wesley had all these long
before they had faith. If there is to be faith, however,
there must be a foundation of knowledge : a man
must know of Christ, and of His cross, and of His
promises, before saving faith becomes a possibility
for him. In our presentation of the gospel, therefore,
we need to stress these things, in order to lead sinners
to abandon all confidence in themselves and to trust
wholly in Christ and the power of His redeeming
blood to give them acceptance with God. For nothing less than this is faith.

(ii) The demand is for *repentance as well as faith*.
It is not enough to believe that only through Christ
and His death are sinners justified and accepted, and

that one's own record is sufficient to bring down
God's condemning sentence twenty times over, and
that, apart from Christ, one has no hope. Knowledge
of the gospel, and orthodox belief of it, is no substitute for repentance. If there is to be repentance,
however, there must, again, be a foundation of
knowledge. A man must know that, in the words of
the first of Luther's Ninety-five Theses, 'when our
Lord and Master, Jesus Christ, said "Repent", He
called for the entire life of believers to be one of
repentance,' and he must also know what repentance
involves. More than once, Christ deliberately called
attention to the radical break with the past that
repentance involves. 'If any man will come after me,
let him *deny himself*, and take up his cross daily,
and follow me . . . whosoever will *lose his life for my
sake*, the same (but only he) shall save it.'[5] 'If any
man come to me, and *hate not* his father, and
mother, and wife, and children, and brethren, and
sisters, yea, and his own life also (*i.e.*, put them all
decisively second in his esteem), *he cannot be my
disciple* . . . whosoever he be of you that forsaketh
not all that he hath, *he cannot be my disciple*.'[6] The
repentance that Christ requires of His people consists
in a settled refusal to set any limit to the claims
which He may make on their lives. Our Lord knew
—who better?—how costly His followers would find
it to maintain this refusal, and let Him have His
way with them all the time, and therefore He wished
them to face out and think through the implications
of discipleship before committing themselves. He

[5] Lk. ix.23 f.   [6] Lk. xiv.26, 33.

did not desire to make disciples under false pretences. He had no interest in gathering vast crowds of professed adherents who would melt away as soon as they found out what following Him actually demanded of them. In our own presentation of Christ's gospel, therefore, we need to lay a similar stress on the cost of following Christ, and make sinners face it soberly before we urge them to respond to the message of free forgiveness. In common honesty, we must not conceal the fact that free forgiveness in one sense will cost everything; or else our evangelizing becomes a sort of confidence trick. And where there is no clear knowledge, and hence no realistic recognition of the real claims that Christ makes, there can be no repentance, and therefore no salvation.

Such is the evangelistic message that we are sent to make known.

III. WHAT IS THE MOTIVE FOR EVANGELIZING?

There are, in fact, two motives that should spur us constantly to evangelize. The first is love to God and concern for His glory; the second is love to man and concern for his welfare.

1. The *first* motive is primary and fundamental. The chief end of man is to glorify God. The biblical rule of life is: 'do all to the glory of God.'[7] Men glorify God by obeying His word and fulfilling His revealed will. Similarly, the first and great commandment is: 'Thou shalt love the Lord thy God.'[8] We show love to the Father and the Son, who have so richly loved us, by keeping Their commandments.

[7] I Cor. x.31.   [8] Mt. xxii.37 f.

'He that hath my commandments, and keepeth them, he it is that loveth me,' said our Lord.[9] 'This is the love of God,' wrote John, 'that we keep his commandments.'[1] Now, evangelism is one of the activities that the Father and the Son have commanded. 'This gospel of the kingdom,' Christ tells us, 'shall' (according to Mark, 'must') 'be preached in all the world for a witness.'[2] And before His ascension Christ charged His disciples in the following categorical terms : 'Go ye . . . and make disciples of all the nations.' To this command He added at once a comprehensive promise : 'and lo, I am with you alway, even unto the end of the world.'[3] The comprehensiveness of this promise shows us how wide is the application of the command to which it is appended. The phrase 'even unto the end of the world' makes it clear that the 'you' to whom the promise was given was not solely and exclusively the eleven disciples; this promise extends to the whole Christian Church throughout history, the entire community of which the eleven were, so to speak, founder members. It is, therefore, a promise for us no less than for them, and a promise of great comfort too. But if the promise extends to us, then the commission with which it is linked must extend to us also. The promise was given to encourage the eleven, lest they be overwhelmed at the size and difficulty of the task of world evangelism that Christ was laying upon them. If it is our privilege to appropriate the promise, then it is also our responsibility to accept the

   [9] Jn. xiv.21.   [1] I Jn. v.3.
 [2] Mt. xxiv.14; Mk. xiii.10.   [3] Mt. xxviii.19 f., RV.

commission. The task laid upon the eleven is the Church's constant task. And if it is the Church's task in general, then it is your task and my task in particular. If, therefore, we love God and are concerned to glorify Him, we must obey His command to evangelize.

There is a further strand to this thought. We glorify God by evangelizing, not only because evangelizing is an act of obedience, but also because in evangelism we tell the world what great things God has done for the salvation of sinners. God is glorified when His mighty works of grace are made known. The psalmist exhorts us to 'shew forth his salvation from day to day. Declare his glory among the heathen, his wonders among all people.'[4] For a Christian to talk to the unconverted about the Lord Jesus Christ and His saving power is in itself honouring and glorifying to God.

2. The *second* motive that should prompt us to assiduous evangelism is love to our neighbour, and the desire to see our fellow-men saved. The wish to win the lost for Christ should be, and indeed is, the natural, spontaneous outflow of love in the heart of everyone who has been born again. Our Lord confirms the Old Testament demand that we should love our neighbour as ourselves.[5] 'As we have therefore opportunity,' writes Paul, 'let us do good unto all men.'[6] What greater need has any man than the need to know Christ? What greater good can we do to any man than to set before him the knowledge of Christ? Insofar as we really love our neighbour as

'Ps. xcvi.2 f.   [5] Mk. xii.31; Lk. x.27 f.   [6] Gal. vi.10.

ourselves, we shall of necessity want him to enjoy the
salvation which is so precious to us. This, indeed,
should not be a thing that we need to think about,
let alone argue about. The impulse to evangelize
should spring up spontaneously in us as we see our
neighbour's need of Christ.

Who is my neighbour? When the lawyer, confronted with the demand of love for one's neighbour,
asked our Lord this question, Christ replied by tell-
ing the story of the Good Samaritan.[7] What that
story teaches is simply this : that any fellow human
being whom you meet who is in need is your neighbour; God has put him there so that you may help
him; and your business is to show yourself neighbour
to him by doing all that you can to meet his need,
whatever it may be. 'Go, and do thou likewise,' said
our Lord to the lawyer. He says the same to us. And
the principle applies to all forms of need, spiritual
no less than material. So that when we find ourselves
in contact with men and women who are without
Christ, and so face spiritual death, we are to look on
them as our neighbours in this sense, and ask ourselves what we can do to make Christ known to
them.

May I stress again : if we ourselves have known
anything of the love of Christ for us, and if our
hearts have felt any measure of gratitude for the
grace that has saved us from death and hell, then
this attitude of compassion and care for our spiritually needy fellow-men ought to come naturally and
spontaneously to us. It was in connection with

[7] Lk. x.29 ff.

aggressive evangelism that Paul declared that 'the love of Christ constraineth us'.[8] It is a tragic and ugly thing when Christians lack desire, and are actually reluctant, to share the precious knowledge that they have with others whose need of it is just as great as their own. It was natural for Andrew, when he found the Messiah, to go off and tell his brother Simon, and for Philip to hurry to break the good news to his friend Nathanael.[9] They did not need to be told to do this; they did it naturally and spontaneously, just as one would naturally and spontaneously share with one's family and friends any other piece of news that vitally affected them. There is something very wrong with us if we do not ourselves find it natural to act in this way : let us be quite clear about that. It is a great privilege to evangelize; it is a wonderful thing to be able to tell others of the love of Christ, knowing that there is nothing that they need more urgently to know, and no knowledge in the world that can do them so much good. We should not, therefore, be reluctant and backward to evangelize on the personal and individual level. We should be glad and happy to do it. We should not look for excuses for wriggling out of our obligation when occasion offers to talk to others about the Lord Jesus Christ. If we find ourselves shrinking from this responsibility, and trying to evade it, we need to face ourselves with the fact that in this we are yielding to sin and Satan. If (as is usual) it is the fear of being thought odd and ridiculous, or of losing popularity in certain circles, that holds us back, we need to ask

[8] 2 Cor. v.14.   [9] Jn. i.40 ff.

ourselves in the presence of God : Ought these things
to stop us loving our neighbour ? If it is a false shame,
which is not shame at all, but pride in disguise, that
keeps our tongue from Christian witness when we
are with other people, we need to press upon our
conscience this question : Which matters more—our
reputation, or their salvation? We cannot be complacent about this gangrene of conceit and coward-
ice when we weigh up our lives in the presence of
God. What we need to do is to ask for grace to be
truly ashamed of ourselves, and to pray that we may
so overflow in love to God that we shall overflow in
love to our fellow-men, and so find it an easy and
natural and joyful thing to share with them the good
news of Christ.

By now, I hope, it is becoming clear to us how we
should regard our evangelistic responsibility. Evangelism is not the only task that our Lord has given
us, nor is it a task that we are all called to discharge in
the same way. We are not all called to be preachers;
we are not all given equal opportunities or compar-
able abilities for personal dealing with men and
women who need Christ. But we all have some evangelistic responsibility which we cannot shirk without
failing in love both to our God and to our neighbour.
To start with, we all can and should be praying for
the salvation of unconverted people, particularly in
our family, and among our friends and everyday
associates. And then we must learn to see what possibilities of evangelism our everyday situation holds,
and to be enterprising in our use of them. It is
the nature of love to be enterprising. If you love

someone, you are constantly trying to think out what is the best you can do for him, and how best you can please him, and it is your pleasure to give him pleasure by the things you devise for him. If, then, we love God—Father, Son, and Spirit—for all that They have done for us, we shall muster all our initiative and enterprise to make the most that we can of every situation for Their glory—and one chief way of doing this is to seek out ways and means of spreading the gospel, and obeying the divine command to make disciples everywhere. Similarly, if we love our neighbour, we shall muster all our initiative and enterprise to find ways and means of doing him good. And one chief way of doing him good is to share with him our knowledge of Christ. Thus, if we love God and our neighbour, we shall evangelize, and we shall be enterprising in our evangelism. We shall not ask with reluctance how much we have to do in this realm, as if evangelizing were a distasteful and burdensome task. We shall not enquire anxiously after the minimum outlay of effort in evangelism that will satisfy God. But we shall ask eagerly, and pray earnestly to be shown, just how much it is in our power to do to spread the knowledge of Christ among men; and once we see what the possibilities are, we shall give ourselves wholeheartedly to the task.

One further point must be added, however, lest what we have said be misapplied. It must never be forgotten that the enterprise required of us in evangelism is the enterprise of love: an enterprise that springs from a genuine interest in those whom we seek to win, and a genuine care for their well-being, and expresses itself in a genuine respect for them and a genuine friendliness towards them. One sometimes meets a scalp-hunting zeal in evangelism, both in the pulpit and on the personal level, which is both discreditable and alarming. It is discreditable, because it reflects, not love and care, nor the desire to be of help, but arrogance, and conceit, and pleasure in having power over the lives of others. It is alarming, because it finds expression in a ferocious psychological pommelling of the poor victim which may do great damage to sensitive and impressionable souls. But if love prompts and rules our evangelistic work, we shall approach other people in a different spirit. If we truly care for them, and if our heart truly loves and fears God, then we shall seek to present Christ to them in a way that is both honouring to Him and respectful to them. We shall not try to violate their personalities, or exploit their weaknesses, or ride roughshod over their feelings. What we shall be trying to do, rather, is to show them the reality of our friendship and concern by sharing with them our most valuable possession. And this spirit of friendship and concern will shine through all that we say to them, whether in the pulpit or in private, however drastic and shattering the truths that we tell them may be.

There is a famous old book on personal evangelism by C. G. Trumbull, entitled *Taking Men Alive*. In the third chapter of that book, the author tells us of the rule that his father, H. C. Trumbull, made for himself in this matter. It was as follows:

'Whenever I am justified in choosing my subject of
conversation with another, the theme of themes
(Christ) shall have prominence between us, so that I
may learn of his need, and, if possible, meet it.' The
key words here are: *'whenever I am justified in
choosing my subject of conversation with another'*.
They remind us, first, that personal evangelism, like
all our dealings with our fellow-men, should be
courteous. And they remind us, second, that personal
evangelism needs normally to be founded on friendship. You are not usually justified in choosing the
subject of conversation with another till you have
already begun to give yourself to him in friendship
and established a relationship with him in which he
feels that you respect him, and are interested in him,
and are treating him as a human being, and not just
as some kind of 'case'. With some people, you may
establish such a relationship in five minutes, whereas
with others it may take months. But the principle
remains the same. The right to talk intimately to
another person about the Lord Jesus Christ has to
be earned, and you earn it by convincing him that
you are his friend, and really care about him. And
therefore the indiscriminate buttonholing, the in-
trusive barging in to the privacy of other people's
souls, the thick-skinned insistence on expounding the
things of God to reluctant strangers who are longing
to get away—these modes of behaviour, in which
strong and loquacious personalities have sometimes
indulged in the name of personal evangelism, should
be written off as a travesty of personal evangelism.
Impersonal evangelism would be a better name for

them! In fact, rudeness of this sort dishonours God;
moreover, it creates resentment, and prejudices
people against the Christ whose professed followers
act so objectionably. The truth is that real personal
evangelism is very costly, just because it demands of
us a really personal relationship with the other man.
We have to give ourselves in honest friendship to
people, if ever our relationship with them is to reach
the point at which we are justified in choosing to talk
to them about Christ, and can speak to them about
their own spiritual needs without being either dis-
courteous or offensive. If you wish to do personal
evangelism, then—and I hope you do; you ought to
—pray for the gift of friendship. A genuine friendliness is in any case a prime mark of the man who
is learning to love his neighbour as himself.

IV. BY WHAT MEANS AND METHODS SHOULD
EVANGELISM BE PRACTISED?

There is today a controversy in some evangelical
circles about evangelistic methods. Some are criticiz-
ing, and others are defending, the type of evangelistic meeting that has been a standard feature of
English and American evangelical life for almost a
century. Meetings of this type are well known, for
they are very characteristic. They are deliberately
made brisk and bright, in the hope that people who
have little interest in the Christian message, and who
may never have been inside a Christian church, may
nevertheless find them an attraction. Everything is
accordingly planned to create an atmosphere of

warmth, good humour and happiness. The meeting normally includes a good deal of music—choir items, solo items, choruses, and rousing hymns, heartily sung. Heavy emphasis is laid on the realities of Christian experience, both by the choice of hymns and by the use of testimonies. The meeting leads up to an appeal for decision, followed by an after-meeting or a time of personal counselling for the further instruction of those who have made, or wish to make, a decision in response to the appeal.

The main criticisms that are made of such meetings—whether they are wholly justified we would not venture to say—are as follows. Their breezy slickness (it is said) makes for irreverence. The attempt to give them 'entertainment value' tends to lessen the sense of God's majesty, to banish the spirit of worship, and to cheapen men's thoughts of their Creator; moreover, it is the worst possible preparation of the potential converts for the regular Sunday services in the churches which they will in due course join. The seemingly inevitable glamourizing of Christian experience in the testimonies is pastorally irresponsible, and gives a falsely romanticized impression of what being a Christian is like. This, together with the tendency to indulge in long-drawn-out wheedling for decisions and the deliberate use of luscious music to stir sentiment, tends to produce 'conversions' which are simply psychological and emotional upheavals, and not the fruit of spiritual conviction and renewal at all. The occasional character of the meetings makes it inevitable that appeals for decision will often be made on the

basis of inadequate instruction as to what the decision involves and will cost, and such appeals are no
better than a confidence trick. The desire to justify
the meetings by reaping a crop of converts may
prompt the preacher and the counsellors to try and
force people through the motions of decision prema-
turely, before they have grasped what it is really all
about, and converts produced in this way tend to
prove at best stunted and at worst spurious and, in
the event, gospel-hardened. The way ahead in evangelism, it is said, is to break completely with this
pattern of evangelistic action, and to develop a new
pattern (or, rather, restore the old one which existed
before this type of meeting became standard), in
which the evangelizing unit is the local church rather
than a group or cross-section of churches, and the
evangelistic meeting finds its place among the local
church's services—a pattern, indeed, in which the
local church's services function continually as its
evangelistic meetings.

The usual reply is that, while the things stigma-
tized are certainly real abuses, evangelistic meetings
of the standard pattern can be, and frequently are,
run in a way that avoids them. Such meetings, it is
said, have proved their usefulness in the past; experience shows that God uses them still; and there seems
to be no sufficient reason for abandoning them. It is
argued that, while so many churches in each major
denomination are failing in their evangelistic responsibility, these meetings may well be the only opportunity for presenting the gospel to vast multitudes of
our fellow-men and women. The way ahead, there-

fore, it is maintained, is not to abolish them, but to reform them where abuses exist.

The debate continues. No doubt it will remain with us for some time to come. What I want to do here is not to go into this controversy, but to go behind it. I want to isolate the key principle that should guide us in our assessment both of these and any other methods of evangelism that may be practised or proposed.

What is this key principle? The following line of thought will make it clear.

Evangelism, as we have seen, is an act of communication with a view to conversion. In the last analysis, therefore, there is only one *means* of evangelism: namely, the gospel of Christ, explained and applied. Faith and repentance, the two complementary elements of which conversion consists, occur as a response to the gospel. 'Belief cometh of hearing,' Paul tells us, 'and hearing by the word of Christ'[1]—or, as *The New English Bible* expands the verse, 'faith is awakened by the message, and the message that awakens it comes through the word of Christ'.

Again, in the last analysis, there is only one *agent* of evangelism: namely, the Lord Jesus Christ. It is Christ Himself who through His Holy Spirit enables His servants to explain the gospel truly and apply it powerfully and effectively; just as it is Christ Himself who through His Holy Spirit opens men's minds[2] and hearts[3] to receive the gospel, and so

[1] Rom. x.17, RV.   [2] Lk. xxiv.45.   [3] Acts xvi.14.

draws them savingly to Himself.[4] Paul speaks of his achievements as an evangelist as 'those (things) which *Christ wrought through me*, for the obedience of the Gentiles, by word and deed . . . *in the power of the Holy Ghost*'.[5] Since Augustine the point has often been made that Christ is the true minister of the gospel sacraments, and the human celebrant acts merely as His hand. We need to remember the equally basic truth that Christ is the true minister of the gospel word, and the human preacher or witness acts merely as His mouth.

So, in the last analysis, there is only one *method* of evangelism: namely, the faithful explanation and application of the gospel message. From which it follows—and this is the key principle which we are seeking—that the test for any proposed strategy, or technique, or style, of evangelistic action must be this: will it in fact serve the word? Is it calculated to be a means of explaining the gospel truly and fully and applying it deeply and exactly? To the extent to which it is so calculated, it is lawful and right; to the extent to which it tends to overlay and obscure the realities of the message, and to blunt the edge of their application, it is ungodly and wrong.

Let us work this out. It means that we need to bring under review all our evangelistic plans and practices—our missions, rallies, and campaigns; our sermons, talks, and testimonies; our big meetings, our little meetings, and our presentation of the gospel in personal dealing; the tracts that we give, the books that we lend, the letters that we write—

[4] Jn. xii.32.   [5] Rom. xv.18 f., RV.

and to ask about each of them questions such as the following:

Is this way of presenting Christ calculated to impress on people that the gospel is *a word from God*? Is it calculated to divert their attention from man and all things merely human to God and His truth? Or is its tendency rather to distract attention from the Author and authority of the message to the person and performance of the messenger? Does it make the gospel sound like a human idea, a preacher's plaything, or like a divine revelation, before which the human messenger himself stands in awe? Does this way of presenting Christ savour of human cleverness and showmanship? Does it tend thereby to exalt man? Or does it embody rather the straightforward, unaffected simplicity of the messenger whose sole concern is to deliver his message, and who has no wish to call attention to himself, and who desires so far as he can to blot himself out and hide, as it were, behind his message, fearing nothing so much as that men should admire and applaud him when they ought to be bowing down and humbling themselves before the mighty Lord whom he represents?

Again: is this way of presenting Christ calculated to promote, or impede, the work of the word in men's *minds*? Is it going to clarify the meaning of the message, or to leave it enigmatic and obscure, locked up in pious jargon and oracular formulae? Is it going to make people think, and think hard, and think hard about God, and about themselves in relation to God? Or will it tend to stifle thought by

playing exclusively on the emotions? Is it calculated to stir the mind, or put it to sleep? Is this way
of presenting Christ an attempt to move men by the
force of feeling, or of truth? Not, of course, that
there is anything wrong with emotion; it is strange
for a person to be converted without emotion; what
is wrong is the sort of appeal to emotion, and playing
on emotion, which harrows people's feelings as a
substitute for instructing their minds.

Again : we have to ask, is this way of presenting
Christ calculated to convey to people the *doctrine* of
the gospel, and not just part of it, but the whole of it
—the truth about our Creator and His claims, and
about ourselves as guilty, lost, and helpless sinners,
needing to be born again, and about the Son of God
who became man, and died for sins, and lives to
forgive sinners and bring them to God? Or is it likely
to be deficient here, and deal in half-truths, and
leave people with an incomplete understanding of
these things, and hurry them on to the demand for
faith and repentance without having made it clear
just what they need to repent of, or what they ought
to believe?

Again : we have to ask, is this way of presenting
Christ calculated to convey to people the *application*
of the gospel, and not just part of it, but the whole
of it—the summons to see and know oneself as God
sees and knows one, that is, as a sinful creature, and
to face the breadth and depth of the need into which
a wrong relationship with God has brought one, and
to face too the cost and consequences of turning to
receive Christ as Saviour and Lord? Or is it likely to

be deficient here, and to gloss over some of this, and to give an inadequate, distorted impression of what the gospel requires? Will it, for instance, leave people unaware that they have any immediate obligation to respond to Christ at all? Or will it leave them supposing that all they have to do is to trust Christ as a sin-bearer, not realizing that they must also deny themselves and enthrone Him as their Lord (the error which we might call only-believism)? Or will it leave them imagining that the whole of what they have to do is to consecrate themselves to Christ as their Master, not realizing that they must also receive Him as their Saviour (the error which we might call good-resolutionism)? We need to remember here that spiritually it is even more dangerous for a man whose conscience is roused to make a misconceived response to the gospel, and take up with a defective religious practice, than for him to make no response at all. If you turn a publican into a Pharisee, you make his condition worse, not better.

Again : we have to ask, is this way of presenting Christ calculated to convey gospel truth in a manner that is appropriately *serious?* Is it calculated to make people feel that they are indeed facing a matter of life and death? Is it calculated to make them see and feel the greatness of God, and the greatness of their sin and need, and the greatness of the grace of Christ? Is it calculated to make them aware of the awful majesty and holiness of God? Will it help them to realize that it is a fearful thing to fall into His hands? Or is this way of presenting Christ so

light and casual and cosy and jolly as to make it
hard for the hearers to feel that the gospel is a matter
of any consequence, save as a pick-me-up for life's
misfits? It is a gross insult to God, and a real dis-
service to men, to cheapen and trivialize the gospel
by one's presentation of it. Not that we should
put on an affected solemnity when speaking of
spiritual things; there is nothing more essentially
frivolous than a mock seriousness, and nothing more
likely to make hypocrites out of our hearers. What is
needed is this : that we, who would speak for Christ,
should pray constantly that God will put and keep in
our hearts a sense of His greatness and glory, and of
the joy of fellowship with Him, and of the dreadful-
ness of spending time and eternity without Him; and
then that God will enable us to speak honestly,
straightforwardly, and just as we feel about these
matters. Then we shall be really natural in presenting the gospel—and really serious too.

It is by asking questions of this sort that we must
test and, where necessary, reform our evangelistic
methods. The principle is that the best method of
evangelism is the one which serves the gospel most
completely. It is the one which bears the clearest
witness to the divine origin of the message, and the
life-and-death character of the issues which it raises.
It is the one which makes possible the most full and
thorough explanation of the good news of Christ and
His cross, and the most exacting and searching
application of it. It is the one which most effectively
engages the minds of those to whom witness is
borne, and makes them most vividly aware that the

gospel is God's word, addressed personally to them in their own situation. What that best method is in each case, you and I have to find out for ourselves. It is in the light of this principle that all debates about evangelistic methods must be decided. For the present, we leave the matter there.

CHAPTER IV

DIVINE SOVEREIGNTY AND EVANGELISM

W E start this final section by summing up what we have learned so far about evangelism.

Evangelism, we have learned, is a task appointed to all God's people everywhere. It is the task of communicating a message from the Creator to rebel mankind. The message begins with information and ends with an invitation. The information concerns God's work of making His Son a perfect Saviour for sinners. The invitation is God's summons to mankind generally to come to the Saviour and find life. God commands all men everywhere to repent, and promises forgiveness and restoration to all who do. The Christian is sent into the world as God's herald and Christ's ambassador, to broadcast this message as widely as he can. This is both his duty (because God commands it, and love to our neighbour requires it) and his privilege (because it is a great thing to speak for God, and to take our neighbour the remedy—the only remedy—that can save him from the terrors of spiritual death). Our job, then, is to go to our fellow-men and tell them the gospel of Christ, and try by every means to make it clear to them; to remove as best we can any difficulties that they may find in it, to impress them with its seriousness, and to urge them to respond to it. This is our abiding responsibility; it is a basic part of our Christian calling.

But now we come to the question that has loomed over us from the outset. How is all this affected by our belief in the sovereignty of God?

We saw earlier that divine sovereignty is one of a pair of truths which form an antinomy in biblical thinking. The God of the Bible is both Lord and Lawgiver in His world; He is both man's King and man's Judge. Consequently, if we would be biblical in our outlook, we have to make room in our minds for the thoughts of divine sovereignty and of human responsibility to stand side by side. Man is indubitably responsible to God, for God is the Lawgiver who fixes his duty, and the Judge who takes account of him as to whether or not he has done it. And God is indubitably sovereign over man, for He controls and orders all human deeds, as He controls and orders all else in His universe. Man's responsibility for his actions, and God's sovereignty in relation to those same actions, are thus, as we saw, equally real and ultimate facts.

The apostle Paul forces this antinomy upon our notice by speaking of God's will (*thelēma*) in connection with both these seemingly incompatible relations of the Creator to His human creatures, and that within the limits of a single short Epistle. In the fifth and sixth chapters of Ephesians, he desires that his readers may be found 'understanding what the *will* of the Lord is' (v. 17) and 'doing the *will* of God from the heart' (vi.6). This is the will of God as Law-

giver, the will of God that man is to know and obey.
In the same sense, Paul writes to the Thessalonians:
'This is the *will* of God, even your sanctification,
that ye should abstain from fornication.'[1] In the first
chapter of Ephesians, however, Paul speaks of God's
having chosen him and his fellow-Christians in
Christ before the world began 'according to the good
pleasure of his *will*' (verse 5); he calls God's intention
to sum up all things in Christ at the end of the world
'the mystery of his *will*' (verse 9); and he speaks of
God Himself as 'him who worketh all things after
the counsel of his own *will*' (verse 11). Here God's
'will' is clearly His eternal purpose for the disposal
of His creatures, His will as the world's sovereign
Lord. This is the will that God actually fulfils in and
through everything that actually happens—even
man's transgressions of His law.[2] Older theology
distinguished the two as God's will of *precept* and
His will of *purpose*, the former being His published
declaration of what man ought to do, the latter His
(largely secret) decision as to what He Himself will
do. The distinction is between God's *law* and His
plan. The former tells man what he should be; the
latter settles what he will be. Both aspects of the will
of God are facts, though how they are related in the
mind of God is inscrutable to us. This is one of the
reasons why we speak of God as incomprehensible.

Now, our question is: Supposing that all things
do in fact happen under the direct dominion of God,

---

[1] 1 Thes. iv.3; *cf.* Mt. vii.21,xii.50;Jn.vii.17; 1 Jn. ii.17, etc.
[2] See, *e.g.*, Gn. xlv.5 ff., l.20. God's *thelema* is spoken of in
this sense in Rom. i.10, xv.32; Rev. iv.11, etc.

and that God has already fixed the future by His decree, and resolved whom He will save, and whom not—how does this bear on our duty to evangelize?

This is a question that troubles many evangelical Christians today. There are some who have come to believe in the sovereignty of God in the unqualified and uncompromising way in which (as we judge) the Bible presents it. These are now wondering whether there is not some way in which they could and should witness to this faith by modifying the evangelistic practice which they have inherited from a generation with different convictions. These methods, they say, were devised by people who did not believe what we believe about God's absolute sovereignty in salvation; is that not of itself reason enough for refusing to use them? Others, who do not construe the doctrine of divine sovereignty in quite this way, nor take it quite so seriously, fear that this new concern to believe it thoroughly will mean the death of evangelism; for they think it is bound to undercut all sense of urgency in evangelistic action. Satan, of course, will do anything to hold up evangelism and divide Christians; so he tempts the first group to become inhibited and cynical about all current evangelistic endeavours, and the second group to lose its head and become panicky and alarmist, and both to grow self-righteous and bitter and conceited as they criticize each other. Both groups, it seems, have urgent need to watch against the wiles of the devil.

The question, then, is pressing. It was the Bible itself that raised it, by teaching the antinomy of God's dual relation to man; and we look now to the Bible to answer it.

The biblical answer may be stated in two propositions, one negative and one positive.

1. *The sovereignty of God in grace does not affect anything that we have said about the nature and duty of evangelism.*

The principle that operates here is that the rule of our duty and the measure of our responsibility is God's revealed will of precept, and not His hidden will of event. We are to order our lives by the light of His law, not by our guesses about His plan. Moses laid down this principle when he had finished teaching Israel the law, the threats, and the promises of the Lord. 'The secret things belong unto the Lord our God: but those things which are revealed belong unto us . . . that we may do all the words of this law.'[3] The things that God is pleased to keep to Himself (the number and identity of the elect, for instance, and when and how He purposes to convert whom) have no bearing on any man's duty. They are not relevant in any way for the interpreting of any part of God's law. Now, the command to evangelize is a part of God's law. It belongs to God's revealed will for His people. It could not, then, in principle be affected in the slightest degree by anything that we might believe about God's sovereignty in election and calling. We may well believe that (in the words of Article XVII of the Church of England) God 'hath constantly (*i.e.*, firmly, decisively) decreed by his counsel secret to us, to deliver from curse and damnation those whom he hath chosen in Christ out of mankind, and to bring them by Christ to everlasting salvation, as vessels made to honour'. But this does not help us to determine the nature of the evangelistic task, nor does it affect our duty to evangelize universally and indiscriminately. The doctrine of God's sovereignty in grace has no bearing on these things.

Therefore we may say:

(i) The belief that God is sovereign in grace does not affect the *necessity* of evangelism. Whatever we may believe about election, the fact remains that evangelism is necessary, because no man can be saved without the gospel. 'There is no difference between the Jew and the Greek,' proclaims Paul; 'for the same Lord over all is rich unto all that call upon him. For whosoever shall call upon the name of the Lord (Jesus Christ) shall be saved.' Yes; but nobody will be saved who does not call upon the name of the Lord, and certain things must happen before any man can do this. So Paul continues: 'How then shall they call on him in whom they have not *believed*? and how shall they believe in him of whom they have not *heard*? and how shall they hear without a *preacher*?'[1] They must be told of Christ before they can trust Him, and they must trust Him before they can be saved by Him. Salvation depends on faith, and faith on knowing the gospel. God's way of saving sinners is to bring them to faith through bringing them into contact with the gospel. In God's

[1] Rom. x.12 ff.

ordering of things, therefore, evangelism is a necessity if anyone is to be saved at all.

We must realize, therefore, that when God sends
us to evangelize, He sends us to act as vital links in
the chain of His purpose for the salvation of His
elect. The fact that He has such a purpose, and that
it is (so we believe) a sovereign purpose that cannot
be thwarted, does not imply that, after all, our
evangelizing is not needed for its fulfilment. In our
Lord's parable, the way in which the wedding was
furnished with guests was through the action of the
king's servants, who went out as they were bidden
into the highways and invited in all whom they
found there. Hearing the invitation, the passers-by
came.[5] It is in the same way, and through similar
action by the servants of God, that the elect come
into the salvation that the Redeemer has won for
them.

(*ii*) The belief that God is sovereign in grace does
not affect the *urgency* of evangelism. Whatever we
may believe about election, the fact remains that
men without Christ are lost, and going to hell
(pardon the use of this tarnished phrase : I use it
because I mean it). 'Except ye repent,' said our Lord
to the crowd, 'ye shall *all* . . . *perish*.'[6] And we who
are Christ's are sent to tell them of the One—the
only One—who can save them from perishing. Is
not their need urgent? If it is, does that not make
evangelism a matter of urgency for us? If you knew
that a man was asleep in a blazing building, you
would think it a matter of urgency to try and get to

him, and wake him up, and bring him out. The world is full of people who are unaware that they stand under the wrath of God : is it not similarly a matter of urgency that we should go to them, and try to arouse them, and show them the way of escape?

We should not be held back by the thought that if they are not elect, they will not believe us, and our efforts to convert them will fail. That is true; but it is none of our business, and should make no difference to our action. In the first place, it is always wrong to abstain from doing good for fear that it might not be appreciated. In the second place, the non-elect in this world are faceless men as far as we are concerned. We know that they exist, but we do not and cannot know who they are, and it is as futile as it is impious for us to try and guess. The identity of the reprobate is one of God's 'secret things' into which His people may not pry. In the third place, our calling as Christians is not to love God's elect, and them only, but to love our neighbour, irrespective of whether he is elect or not. Now, the nature of love is to do good and to relieve need. If, then, our neighbour is unconverted, we are to show love to him as best we can by seeking to share with him the good news without which he must needs perish. So we find Paul warning and teaching 'every man' : [1] not merely because he was an apostle, but because every man was his neighbour. And the measure of the urgency of our evangelistic task is the greatness

[1] Col. i.28.

of our neighbour's need and the immediacy of his danger.

(*iii*) The belief that God is sovereign in grace does not affect the *genuineness* of the gospel invitations, or the *truth* of the gospel promises. Whatever we may believe about election, and, for that matter, about the extent of the atonement, the fact remains that God in the gospel really does offer Christ and promise justification and life to 'whosoever will'. '*Whosoever* shall call upon the name of the Lord shall be saved.'[8] As God commands all men everywhere to repent, so God invites all men everywhere to come to Christ and find mercy. The invitation is for sinners only, but for sinners universally; it is not for sinners of a certain type only, reformed sinners, or sinners whose hearts have been prepared by a fixed minimum of sorrow for sin; but for sinners as such, just as they are. As the hymn puts it:

> 'Let not conscience make you linger,
>   Nor of fitness fondly dream;
> All the fitness He requireth
>   Is to feel your need of Him.'[9]

The fact that the gospel invitation is free and unlimited—'*sinners* Jesus will *receive*'—'come *and welcome* to Jesus Christ'[1]—is the glory of the gospel as a revelation of divine grace.

There is a great moment in the Holy Communion service of the Church of England when the minister

[8] Rom. x.13.
[9] From Joseph Hart's *Come, ye sinners* (*Christian Praise*, 196). The whole hymn is a magnificent statement of the gospel invitation.   [1] Title of a book by John Bunyan.

utters the 'comfortable words'. First the congregation confesses its sins to God in language of extreme strength ('our manifold sins and wickedness . . . provoking most justly thy wrath . . . the burden of them is intolerable. Have mercy upon us, have mercy upon us . . .'). Then the minister turns to face the people and proclaims to them the promises of God.

'Hear what comfortable words our Saviour Christ saith unto *all* that truly turn to him.

'Come unto me *all* that travail and are heavy laden, and I will refresh you.

'So God loved the world, that he gave his only-begotten Son, to the end that *all* that believe in him should not perish, but have everlasting life.

'Hear also what Saint Paul saith.

'This is a true saying, and worthy of *all* men to be received, that Christ Jesus came into the world to save sinners.

'Hear also what Saint John saith.

'If *any man* sin, we have an Advocate with the Father, Jesus Christ the righteous; and he is the propitiation for our sins.'[2]

Why are these words 'comfortable'? Because they are God's words, and they are all true. They are the essential gospel. They are the promises and assurances which Christians who approach the Lord's Table should come trusting. They are the word which the sacrament confirms. Note them carefully. Note first their *substance*. The object of faith which they present is not mere orthodoxy, not mere truth about Christ's atoning death. It is not less than that,

[2] Mt. xi.28; Jn. iii.16; 1 Tim. i.15; 1 Jn. ii.1; italics mine.

but it is more than that. It is the living Christ Himself, the perfect Saviour of sinners, who carries in
Himself all the virtue of His finished work on the
cross. 'Come *unto me . . . He* is the propitiation for
our sins.' These promises direct our trust, not to the
crucifixion as such, but to Christ crucified; not to
His work in the abstract, but to Him who wrought it.
And note second the *universality* of these promises.
They offer Christ to *all* who need him, *all* 'that truly
turn to him', *any man* who has sinned. None are shut
out from mercy save those who shut themselves out
through impenitence and unbelief.

Some fear that a doctrine of eternal election and
reprobation involves the possibility that Christ will
not receive some of those who desire to receive Him,
because they are not elect. The 'comfortable words'
of the gospel promises, however, absolutely exclude
this possibility. As our Lord elsewhere affirmed, in
emphatic and categorical terms : 'Him that cometh
to me I will *in no wise* cast out.'[3]

It is true that God has from all eternity chosen
whom He will save. It is true that Christ came
specifically to save those whom the Father had given
Him. But it is also true that Christ offers Himself
freely to all men as their Saviour, and guarantees to
bring to glory everyone who trusts in Him as such.
See how He Himself deliberately juxtaposes these
two thoughts in the following passage :

'I came down from heaven, not to do mine own
will, but the will of him that sent me. And this is the
Father's will which hath sent me, that of *all which*

* Jn. vi.37.

he hath given me I should lose nothing, but should raise it up again at the last day. And this is the will of him that sent me, that *every one which seeth the Son, and believeth on him,* may have everlasting life : and I will raise him up at the last day.'[4] 'All which he hath given me'—here is Christ's saving mission defined in terms of the whole company of the elect, whom He came specifically to save. 'Every one which seeth the Son, and believeth on him'— here is Christ's saving mission defined in terms of the whole company of lost mankind, to whom He offers Himself without distinction, and whom He will certainly save, if they believe. The two truths stand side by side in these verses, and that is where they belong. They go together. They walk hand in hand. Neither throws doubt on the truth of the other. Neither should fill our minds to the exclusion of the other. Christ means what He says, no less when He undertakes to save all who will trust Him than when He undertakes to save all whom the Father has given Him.

Thus John Owen, the Puritan, who wrote in defence of both unconditional election and limited atonement, is able—is, indeed, constrained—to address the unconverted as follows :

'Consider the infinite condescension and love of Christ, in his invitations and calls of you to come unto him for life, deliverance, mercy, grace, peace and eternal salvation. . . . In the declaration and preaching of them, Jesus Christ yet stands before

[4] Jn. vi. 38 ff.

sinners, calling, inviting, encouraging them to come
unto him.

'This is somewhat of the word which he now
speaks unto you: Why will ye die? why will ye
perish? why will ye not have compassion on your
own souls? Can your hearts endure, or can your
hands be strong, in the day of wrath that is
approaching? . . . Look unto me, and be saved;
come unto me, and I will ease you of all sins, sor-
rows, fears, burdens, and give rest to your souls.
Come, I entreat you; lay aside all procrastinations,
all delays; put me off no more; eternity lies at the
door . . . do not so hate me as that you will rather
perish than accept of deliverance by me.

'These and the like things doth the Lord Christ
continually declare, proclaim, plead and urge upon
the souls of sinners . . . He doth it in the preaching
of the word, as if he were present with you, stood
amongst you, and spake personally to every one of
you . . . He hath appointed the ministers of the
gospel to appear before you, and to deal with you
in his stead, avowing as his own the invitations which
are given you in his name, 2 Cor. v.19, 20.'[5]

So indeed it is. The invitations of Christ are words
of God. They are true. They are meant. They are
genuine invitations. They are to be pressed upon the
unconverted as such. Nothing that we may believe
about God's sovereignty in grace makes any difference to this.

(iv) The belief that God is sovereign in grace does

[5] From *The Glory of Christ* (*Works*, ed. W. Goold, 1850,
I.422).

not affect the *responsibility of the sinner* for his reaction to the gospel. Whatever we may believe about election, the fact remains that a man who rejects Christ thereby becomes the cause of his own condemnation. Unbelief in the Bible is a guilty thing, and unbelievers cannot excuse themselves on the grounds that they were not elect. The unbeliever was really offered life in the gospel, and could have had it if he would; he, and no-one but he, is responsible for the fact that he rejected it, and must now endure the consequences of rejecting it. 'Everywhere in Scripture,' writes Bishop J. C. Ryle, 'it is a leading principle that man can lose his own soul, that if he is lost at last it will be his own fault, and his blood will be on his own head. The same inspired Bible which reveals this doctrine of election is the Bible which contains the words, "Why will ye die, O house of Israel?"—"Ye will not come unto me, that ye might have life."—"This is the condemnation, that light is come into the world, and men loved darkness rather than light, because their deeds were evil." (Ezk. xviii.31; Jn. v.40, iii.19.) The Bible never says that sinners miss heaven because they are not elect, but because they "neglect the great salvation", and because they will not repent and believe. The last judgment will abundantly prove that it is not the want of God's election, so much as laziness, the love of sin, unbelief, and unwillingness to come to Christ, which ruins the souls that are lost.'[6] God gives men what they choose, not the opposite of what they choose. Those who choose death, therefore, have

[6] *Old Paths*, p. 468.

only themselves to thank that God does not give them life. The doctrine of divine sovereignty does not affect the situation in any way.

So much for the first and negative proposition. The second is positive.

2. *The sovereignty of God in grace gives us our only hope of success in evangelism.* Some fear that belief in the sovereign grace of God leads to the conclusion that evangelism is pointless, since God will save His elect anyway, whether they hear the gospel or not. This, as we have seen, is a false conclusion based on a false assumption. But now we must go further, and point out that the truth is just the opposite. So far from making evangelism pointless, the sovereignty of God in grace is the one thing that prevents evangelism from being pointless. For it creates the possibility—indeed, the certainty—that evangelism will be fruitful. Apart from it, there is not even a possibility of evangelism being fruitful. Were it not for the sovereign grace of God, evangelism would be the most futile and useless enterprise that the world has ever seen, and there would be no more complete waste of time under the sun than to preach the Christian gospel.

Why is this? Because of the spiritual inability of man in sin. Let Paul, the greatest of all evangelists, explain this to us.

Fallen man, says Paul, has a blinded mind, and so is unable to grasp spiritual truth. 'The natural (unspiritual, unregenerate) man receiveth not the things of the Spirit of God : for they are foolishness unto him : neither can he know them, because they

are spiritually discerned.'[7] Again, he has a perverse
and ungodly nature. 'The carnal mind (the mind of
the unregenerate man) is enmity against God; for
it is not subject to the law of God, neither indeed can
be.' The consequence? 'So then they that are in the
flesh cannot please God.'[8] In both these passages
Paul makes two distinct statements about fallen man
in relation to God's truth, and the progression of
thought is parallel in both cases. First Paul asserts
unregenerate man's failure, as a matter of fact. He
'receiveth not the things of the Spirit of God'; he 'is
not subject to the law of God'. But then Paul goes
on to interpret his first statement by a second, to the
effect that this failure is a necessity of nature, something certain and inevitable and universal and un-
alterable, just because it is not in man to do otherwise than fail in this way. 'Neither *can* he know
them.' 'Neither indeed *can* be.' Man in Adam has
not got it in him to apprehend spiritual realities, or
to obey God's law from his heart. Enmity against
God, leading to defection from God, is the law of
his nature. It is, so to speak, instinctive to him to
suppress and evade and deny God's truth, and to
shrug off God's authority and to flout God's law
—yes, and when he hears the gospel to disbelieve
and disobey that too. This is the sort of person that
he is. He is, says Paul, '*dead* in trespasses and sins'[9]
—wholly incapacitated for any positive reaction to
God's Word, deaf to God's speech, blind to God's
revelation, impervious to God's inducements. If you
talk to a corpse, there is no response; the man is

[7] I Cor. ii.14.   [8] Rom. viii.7 f.   [9] Eph. ii. 1.

dead. When God's Word is spoken to sinners, there is equally no response; they are 'dead in trespasses and sins'.

Nor is this all. Paul also tells us that Satan (whose power and ill will he never underestimates) is constantly active to keep sinners in their natural state. Satan 'now worketh in the children of disobedience'[1] to ensure that they do not obey God's law. And 'the god of this world hath blinded the minds of them which believe not, lest the light of the glorious gospel of Christ . . . should shine unto them.'[2] So that there are two obstacles in the way of successful evangelism : the first, man's natural and irresistible impulse to oppose God, and the second, Satan's assiduity in shepherding man in the ways of unbelief and disobedience.

What does this mean for evangelism? It means, quite simply, that evangelism, described as we have described it, cannot possibly succeed. However clear and cogent we may be in presenting the gospel, we have no hope of convincing or converting anyone. Can you or I by our earnest talking break the power of Satan over a man's life? No. Can you or I give life to the spiritually dead? No. Can we hope to convince sinners of the truth of the gospel by patient explanation? No. Can we hope to move men to obey the gospel by any words of entreaty that we may utter? No. Our approach to evangelism is not realistic till we have faced this shattering fact, and let it make its proper impact on us. When a schoolmaster is trying to teach children arithmetic, or

---

[1] Eph. ii.2.   [2] 2 Cor. iv.4.

grammar, and finds them slow to learn, he assures himself that the penny must drop sooner or later, and so encourages himself to keep on trying. We can most of us muster great reserves of patience if we think that there is some prospect of ultimate success in what we are attempting. But in the case of evangelism there is no such prospect. Regarded as a human enterprise, evangelism is a hopeless task. It cannot in principle produce the desired effect. We can preach, and preach clearly and fluently and attractively; we can talk to individuals in the most pointed and challenging way; we can organize special services, and distribute tracts, and put up posters, and flood the country with publicity—and there is not the slightest prospect that all this outlay of effort will bring a single soul home to God. Unless there is some other factor in the situation, over and above our own endeavours, all evangelistic action is foredoomed to failure. This is the fact, the brute, rock-bottom fact, that we have to face.

Here, I suspect, we find the canker that is really weakening evangelism in evangelical circles today. Everyone seems to agree that our evangelism is not in a healthy state, but there is no agreement as to the nature of the malady, or what should be done to cure it. Some, as we have indicated, appear to think that the basic trouble is the current revival in many places of faith in the sovereignty of divine grace—a faith which finds expression in a fresh emphasis on the doctrines of unconditional election and effectual calling. Their remedy, it seems, would be to try and refute, or suppress, these doctrines, and

to discourage people from taking them seriously.
Since, however, so many of the greatest evangelists
and missionaries of past days have held precisely
these doctrines, it is, to say the least, not obvious that
the diagnosis is right, or the suggested remedy
appropriate. Moreover, it seems clear that evangelism was languishing between the two world wars,
long before this fresh emphasis began to be made.
Others, as we have also hinted, appear to locate the
trouble in the kind of evangelistic meetings that are
commonly held, and to think that if we cut out the
jollity and made them more sombre, and abolished
appeals and counselling rooms and after-meetings,
our evangelism would automatically be reinvigor-
ated. But this also is not obvious. I suspect that the
root of the trouble with our evangelism today lies
deeper than either of these diagnoses goes. I suspect
that what is really responsible for this sense of evangelistic malaise is a widespread neurosis of disillusionment, an unacknowledged failure of nerve,
springing from a long-standing failure to reckon
with the fact that evangelism, regarded as a human
enterprise, must be expected to fail. Let me explain.

For about a century now, it has been characteristic of evangelical Christians (rightly or wrongly—
we need not discuss that here) to think of evangelism
as a specialized activity, best done in short sharp
bursts ('missions' or 'campaigns'), and needing for its
successful practice a distinctive technique, both for
preaching and for individual dealing. At an early
stage in this period, Evangelicals fell into the way of
assuming that evangelism was sure to succeed if it

was regularly prayed for and correctly run (*i.e.*, if
the distinctive technique was used). This was because in those early days, under men like Moody,
Torrey, Haslam and Hay Aitken, evangelistic campaigns usually were successful—not because they
were always well planned and run (by twentieth-
century standards, they often were not), but because
God was working in Britain in those days in a way
in which He is evidently not working now. Even
then, however, it was noticeable that the second
mission in any place would rarely be as productive
as the first, or the third as the second. But during the
past fifty years, as our country has drifted further
and further from its Christian moorings, the law of
diminishing returns has set in much more drastically.
Evangelistic campaigns have become less and less
fruitful. And this fact has unnerved us.

Why has it unnerved us? Because we were not
prepared for it. We had come to take it for granted
that good organization and efficient technique,
backed by a routine of prayers, was itself sufficient
to guarantee results. We felt that there was an almost
magical potency in the special meeting, the special
choir and soloist, and the special preacher. We felt
convinced that the thing that would always bring
life into a dead church, or a dead town, was a an
intensive evangelistic mission. With the top of our
minds, many of us still think that, or profess to think
it. We tell each other that it is so, and make our
plans on this basis. But with the bottom of our minds,
in our heart of hearts, we have grown discouraged,
and disillusioned, and apprehensive. Once we

thought that well-planned evangelism was sure to succeed, but now we find ourselves afraid each time that it is going to fail, as it has failed so often before. Yet we are afraid to admit our fears to ourselves, for we do not know what to make of a situation in which our planned evangelism fails. So we repress our fears, and our disillusionment becomes a paralysing neurosis, and our evangelistic practice becomes a jaded and half-hearted routine. Basically, the trouble is our unconfessed doubts as to the worthwhileness of what we are doing.

Why have we these doubts? Because we have been disillusioned. How have we been disillusioned? By the repeated failure of the evangelistic techniques in which we once reposed such confidence. What is the cure of our disillusionment? First, we must admit that we were silly ever to think that any evangelistic technique, however skilful, could of itself guarantee conversions; second, we must recognize that, because man's heart is impervious to the word of God, it is no cause for surprise if at any time our evangelism fails to result in conversions; third, we must remember that the terms of our calling are that we should be faithful, not that we should be successful; fourth, we must learn to rest all our hopes of fruit in evangelism upon the omnipotent grace of God.

For God does what man cannot do. God works by His Spirit through His Word in the hearts of sinful men to bring them to repentance and faith. Faith is a gift of God. 'Unto you *it is given* in the behalf of Christ . . . to believe on him,' writes Paul to the

Philippians.[3] 'By grace are ye saved through faith,' he tells the Ephesians, 'and that not of yourselves; it is *the gift of God*.'[4] So, too, repentance is the gift of God. 'Him (Christ) did God exalt,' Peter told the Sanhedrin, '. . . to be a Prince and a Saviour, for to *give* repentance to Israel, and remission of sins.'[5] When the Jerusalem church heard how Peter had been sent to evangelize Cornelius, and how Cornelius had come to faith, they said: 'Then hath God also to the Gentiles *granted* repentance unto life.'[6] You and I cannot make sinners repent and believe in Christ by our words alone; but God works faith and repentance in men's hearts by His Holy Spirit.

Paul terms this God's work of 'calling'. The old theologians named it 'effectual calling', to distinguish it from the ineffective summons that is given when the gospel is preached to a man in whose heart God is not at work. It is the operation whereby God causes sinners to understand and respond to the gospel invitation. It is a work of creative power: by it, God gives men new hearts, freeing them from slavery to sin, abolishing their inability to know and do God's truth, and leading them actually to turn to God and trust Christ as their Saviour. By it, also, God breaks Satan's hold upon them, delivering them from the domain of darkness and transferring them into 'the kingdom of his dear Son'.[7] It is thus a calling that creates the response which it seeks, and

[3] Phil. i.29.
[4] Eph. ii.8. Whether the gift of God in this text is the act of believing, or the fact of being-saved-through-believing (commentators divide), does not affect our point.
[5] Acts v.31, RV.   [6] Acts xi.18.   [7] Col. i.13.

confers the blessing to which it invites. It is often termed the work of 'prevenient grace', because it precedes any motion Godward in the heart of sinful man. It has been described (perhaps misleadingly) as a work of 'irresistible grace', simply because it effectively dethrones the disposition to resist grace. The Westminster Confession analyses it as an activity of God in and upon fallen men, 'enlightening their minds spiritually and savingly to understand the things of God; taking away their heart of stone, and giving unto them an heart of flesh; renewing their wills, and by his almighty power determining them to that which is good; and effectually drawing them to Jesus Christ; yet so as they come most freely, being made willing by his grace.'[8]

Christ Himself taught the universal *necessity* of this calling by the Word and the Spirit. '*No man* can come to me, except the Father which hath sent me draw him.'[9] He also taught the universal *efficacy* of it. '*Every man* . . . that hath heard, and hath learned of the Father, cometh unto me.'[1] And with this He taught the universal *certainty* of it for all whom God has chosen. '*All* that the Father giveth me shall come to me :'[2] they shall hear of Me, and they shall be moved to trust Me. This is the Father's purpose, and the Son's promise.

Paul speaks of this 'effectual calling' as the outworking of God's purpose of election. To the Romans, he says: 'Whom (God) did foreknow, he

[8] Westminster Confession, X.i; *cf.* 2 Cor. iv.6; 1 Cor. ii.10 ff.; Ezk. xxxvi.26 f.; Jn. vi.44 f.; Phil. ii.13.
    [9] Jn. vi.44.   [1] Verse 45.   [2] Verse 37.

also did predestinate to be conformed to the image of his Son . . . moreover whom he did predestinate, them he also *called*: and whom he *called*, them he also justified: and whom he justified, them he also glorified.'[3] To the Thessalonians he writes: 'God hath from the beginning chosen you to salvation through sanctification of the Spirit and belief of the truth: whereunto he *called* you by our gospel, to the obtaining of the glory of our Lord Jesus Christ.'[4] The author of the call, the apostle tells us, is God; the mode of calling is by the gospel; and the issue of the call is a title to glory.

But if this is so, then we see at once why it was that Paul, who faced so realistically the fact of fallen man's slavery to sin and Satan, was able to avoid the disillusionment and discouragement that we feel today as it dawns upon us more and more clearly that, humanly speaking, evangelism is a hopeless task. The reason was that Paul kept his eyes firmly fixed on the sovereignty of God in grace. He knew that God had long before declared that 'my word . . . that goeth forth out of my mouth . . . shall not return unto me void, but it shall accomplish that which I please, and it shall prosper in the thing whereto I sent it.'[5] He knew that this was no less true of the gospel than of any other divine utterance. He knew, therefore, that his own preaching of the gospel would not in the long run prove fruitless. God would see to that. He knew that wherever the word of the gospel went, God would raise the dead. He knew that the word would prove a savour of life to

[3] Rom. viii.29 f.   [4] 2 Thes. ii.13 f.   [5] Is. lv.11.

some of those who heard it. This knowledge made
him confident, tireless, and expectant in his evangelism. And if there were on occasion hard spells,
with much opposition and little visible fruit, he did
not panic or lose heart. For he knew that if Christ
had opened the door for him to make known the
gospel in a place, that meant that it was Christ's
purpose to draw sinners to Himself in that place.
The word would not return void. His business,
therefore, was to be patient and faithful in spreading the good news till the time of harvest should
come.

There was a time at Corinth when things were
hard; there had been some converts, certainly, but
opposition was mounting and even Paul, the daunt-
less, was wondering whether it was worth persevering there. 'Then,' we are told, 'spake the Lord
(Jesus) to Paul in the night by a vision, Be not
afraid, but speak, and hold not thy peace : for I am
with thee, and no man shall set on thee to hurt thee :
for I have much people in this city.'[6] As if to say :
go on preaching and teaching, Paul, and let nothing
stop you; there are many here whom I mean to
bring to Myself through your testimony to My
gospel. 'This confirms S. Luke's emphasis upon the
prevenient choice of God,' comments Rackham.[7]
And Luke's emphasis reflects Paul's conviction,
based upon Christ's own assurance to him. Thus the
sovereignty of God in grace gave Paul hope of success as he preached to deaf ears, and held up Christ

[6] Acts xviii.9 f.
[7] *The Acts of the Apostles*, p. 327; *cf.* Acts xiii.48.

before blind eyes, and sought to move stony hearts. His confidence was that where Christ sends the gospel there Christ has His people—fast bound at present in the chains of sin, but due for release at the appointed moment through a mighty renewing of their hearts as the light of the gospel shines into their darkness, and the Saviour draws them to Himself.

In a great hymn which he wrote shortly after his conversion (possibly the day after), Charles Wesley spoke of what had happened like this:

> 'Long my imprisoned spirit lay
>   Fast bound in sin and nature's night;
> Thine eye diffused a quickening ray,—
>   I woke, the dungeon flamed with light;
> My chains fell off, my heart was free,
> I rose, went forth, and followed thee.'[8]

That is not only a vivid statement of experience; it is also a piece of excellent theology. This is precisely what happens to unconverted men and women wherever the gospel is preached. Paul knew that; hence his confidence and expectancy when evangelizing.

Paul's confidence should be our confidence too. We may not trust in our methods of personal dealing or running evangelistic services, however excellent we may think them. There is no magic in methods, not even in theologically impeccable methods. When we evangelize, our trust must be in God who raises the dead. He is the almighty Lord who turns men's hearts, and He will give conversions

[8] From *And can it be* (*Christian Praise*, 235).

in His own time. Meanwhile, our part is to be faithful in making the gospel known, sure that such labour will never be in vain. This is how the truth of the sovereignty of God's grace bears upon evangelism.

What effects should this confidence and certainty have upon our attitude when evangelizing? Three at least.

(i) It should make us *bold*. It should keep us from being daunted when we find, as we often do, that people's first reaction to the gospel is to shrug it off in apathy or even contempt. Such a reaction should not surprise us; it is only to be expected from the bondslaves of sin and Satan. Nor should it discourage us; for no heart is too hard for the grace of God. Paul was a bitter opponent of the gospel, but Christ laid His hand on Paul, and Paul was broken down and born again. You yourself, since you became a Christian, have been learning constantly how corrupt and deceitful and perverse your own heart is; before you became a Christian, your heart was worse; yet Christ has saved you, and that should be enough to convince you that He can save anyone. So persevere in presenting Christ to unconverted people as you find opportunity. You are not on a fool's errand. You are not wasting either your time or theirs. You have no reason to be ashamed of your message, or half-hearted and apologetic in delivering it. You have every reason to be bold, and free, and natural, and hopeful of success. For God can give His truth an effectiveness that you and I cannot give it. God can make His truth triumphant to the conversion of the most seemingly hardened unbeliever. You and I will never write off anyone as hopeless and beyond the reach of God if we believe in the sovereignty of His grace.

(ii) This confidence should make us *patient*. It should keep us from being daunted when we find that our evangelistic endeavours meet with no immediate response. God saves in His own time, and we ought not to suppose that He is in such a hurry as we are. We need to remember that we are all children of our age, and the spirit of our age is a spirit of tearing hurry. And it is a pragmatic spirit; it is a spirit that demands quick results. The modern ideal is to achieve more and more by doing less and less. This is the age of the labour-saving device, the efficiency chart, and automation. The attitude which all this breeds is one of impatience towards everything that takes time and demands sustained effort. Ours tends to be a slapdash age; we resent spending time doing things thoroughly. This spirit tends to infect our evangelism (not to speak of other departments of our Christianity), and with disastrous results. We are tempted to be in a great hurry with those whom we would win to Christ, and then, when we see no immediate response in them, to become impatient and downcast, and then to lose interest in them, and feel that it is useless to spend more time on them; and so we abandon our efforts forthwith, and let them drop out of our ken. But this is utterly wrong. It is a failure both of love for man and of faith in God.

The truth is that the work of evangelizing demands

more patience and sheer 'stickability', more reserves of persevering love and care, than most of us twentieth-century Christians have at command. It is a work in which quick results are not promised; it is a work, therefore, in which the non-appearance of quick results is no sign of failure; but it is a work in which we cannot hope for success unless we are prepared to persevere with people. The idea that a single evangelistic sermon, or a single serious conversation, ought to suffice for the conversion of anyone who is ever going to be converted is really silly. If you see someone whom you meet come to faith through a single such sermon or talk, you will normally find that his heart was already well prepared by a good deal of Christian teaching and exercise of spirit prior to your meeting with him. The law that operates in such cases is 'one soweth, and another reapeth'.[9] If, on the other hand, you meet a person who is not thus prepared, a person who as yet has no conviction of the truth of the gospel and perhaps no idea, or even a false idea, of what the gospel actually is, it is worse than useless to try and stampede him into a snap 'decision'. You may be able to bully him into a psychological crisis of some sort, but that will not be saving faith, and will do him no good. What you have to do is to take time with him, to make friends with him, to get alongside him, to find out where he is in terms of spiritual understanding, and to start dealing with him at that point. You have to explain the gospel to him, and be sure that he understands it and is con-

[9] Jn. iv.37.

vinced of its truth, before you start pressing him to an active response. You have to be ready to help him, if need be, through a spell of seeking to repent and believe before he knows within himself that he has received Christ, and Christ has received him. At each stage you have to be willing to go along with him at God's speed, which may seem to you a strangely slow speed. But that is God's business, not yours. Your business is simply to keep pace with what God is doing in his life. Your willingness to be patient with him in this way is the proof of your love to him no less than of your faith in God. If you are not willing thus to be patient, you need not expect that God will favour you by enabling you to win souls.

Whence comes the patience that is so indispensable for evangelistic work? From dwelling on the fact that God is sovereign in grace and that His word does not return to Him void; that it is He who gives us such opportunities as we find for sharing our knowledge of Christ with others, and that He is able in His own good time to enlighten them and bring them to faith. God often exercises our patience in this, as in other matters. As He kept Abraham waiting twenty-five years for the birth of his son, so He often keeps Christians waiting for things that they long to see, such as the conversion of their friends. We need patience, then, if we are to do our part in helping others towards faith. And the way for us to develop that patience is to learn to live in terms of our knowledge of the free and gracious sovereignty of God.

(iii) Finally, this confidence should make us *prayerful.*

Prayer, as we said at the beginning, is a confessing of impotence and need, an acknowledging of helplessness and dependence, and an invoking of the mighty power of God to do for us what we cannot do for ourselves. In evangelism, as we saw, we are impotent; we depend wholly upon God to make our witness effective; only because He is able to give men new hearts can we hope that through our preaching of the gospel sinners will be born again. These facts ought to drive us to prayer. It is God's intention that they should drive us to prayer. God means us, in this as in other things, to recognize and confess our impotence, and to tell Him that we rely on Him alone, and to plead with Him to glorify His name. It is His way regularly to withhold His blessings until His people start to pray. 'Ye have not, because ye ask not.'[1] 'Ask, and it shall be given you; seek, and ye shall find; knock, and it shall be opened unto you : for every one that asketh receiveth; and he that seeketh findeth; and to him that knocketh it shall be opened.'[2] But if you and I are too proud or lazy to ask, we need not expect to receive. This is the universal rule, in evangelism as elsewhere. God will make us pray before He blesses our labours in order that we may constantly learn afresh that we depend on God for everything. And then, when God permits us to see conversions, we shall not be tempted to ascribe them to our own gifts, or skill, or wisdom,

[1] Jas. iv.2.   [2] Mt. vii.7 f.

or persuasiveness, but to His work alone, and so we shall know whom we ought to thank for them.

The knowledge, then, that God is sovereign in grace, and that we are impotent to win souls, should make us pray, and keep us praying. What should be the burden of our prayers? We should pray for those whom we seek to win, that the Holy Spirit will open their hearts; and we should pray for ourselves in our own witness, and for all who preach the gospel, that the power and authority of the Holy Spirit may rest upon them. 'Pray for us,' writes Paul to the Thessalonians, 'that the word of the Lord may run and be glorified.'[3] Paul was a great evangelist who had seen much fruit, but Paul knew that every particle of it had come from God, and that unless God continued to work both in him and in those to whom he preached he would never convert another soul. So he pleads for prayer, that his evangelism might still prove fruitful. Pray, he pleads, that the word of the gospel may be glorified through my preaching of it, and through its effect in human lives. Pray that it may be used constantly to the conversion of sinners. This, to Paul, is an urgent request, just because Paul sees so clearly that his preaching can save nobody unless God in sovereign mercy is pleased to bless it and use it to this end. Paul, you see, does not hold that, because God is sovereign in saving sinners, therefore prayer is needless, any more than he holds that, because God is sovereign in saving sinners, evangelistic preaching is needless. Rather, he holds that, just because the sal-

[3] 2 Thes. iii.1, RV.

vation of sinners depends wholly upon God, prayer
for the fruitfulness of evangelistic preaching is all
the more necessary. And those today who, with
Paul, believe most strongly that it is the sovereign
agency of God, and that alone, that leads sinners to
Christ, should bear witness to their faith by showing
themselves most constant and faithful and earnest
and persistent in prayer that God's blessing may rest
on the preaching of His word, and that under it
sinners may be born again. This is the final bearing
of belief in the sovereignty of God's grace upon
evangelism.

We said earlier in this chapter that this doctrine
does not in any way reduce or narrow the terms of
our evangelistic commission. Now we see that, so far
from contracting them, it actually expands them.
For it faces us with the fact that there are two sides
to the evangelistic commission. It is a commission,
not only to preach, but also to pray; not only to talk
to men about God, but also to talk to God about
men. Preaching and prayer must go together; our
evangelism will not be according to knowledge, nor
will it be blessed, unless they do. We are to preach,
because without knowledge of the gospel no man
can be saved. We are to pray, because only the
sovereign Holy Spirit in us and in men's hearts can
make our preaching effective to men's salvation, and
God will not send His Spirit where there is no
prayer. Evangelicals are at present busy reforming
their methods of evangelistic preaching, and that is
good. But it will not lead to evangelistic fruitfulness

unless God also reforms our praying, and pours out on us a new spirit of supplication for evangelistic work. The way ahead for us in evangelism is that we should be taught afresh to testify to our Lord and to His gospel, in public and in private, in preaching and in personal dealing, with boldness, patience, power, authority, and love; and that with this we should also be taught afresh to pray for God's blessing on our witness with humility and importunity. It is as simple—and as difficult—as that. When all has been said that has to be said about the reformation of evangelistic methods, it still remains that there is no way ahead but this, and if we do not find this way, we shall not advance.

Thus the wheel of our argument comes full circle. We began by appealing to our practice of prayer as proof of our faith in divine sovereignty. We end by applying our faith in divine sovereignty as a motive to the practice of prayer.

What, then, are we to say about the suggestion that a hearty faith in the absolute sovereignty of God is inimical to evangelism? We are bound to say that anyone who makes this suggestion thereby shows that he has simply failed to understand what the doctrine of divine sovereignty means. Not only does it undergird evangelism, and uphold the evangelist, by creating a hope of success that could not otherwise be entertained; it also teaches us to bind together preaching and prayer; and as it makes us bold and confident before men, so it makes us humble and importunate before God. Is not this as it should be? We would not wish to say that man cannot evangelize at all without coming to terms with this doctrine; but we venture to think that, other things being equal, he will be able to evangelize better for believing it.